Praise for
Life After Law
and **Liz Brown**

"This wonderful book is the answer to the 'Thank-God-it's-Friday' syndrome that affects so many lawyers who dread Monday. Liz Brown shows that you can find work you love. You just have to know where to look. You can do good and do well. You just have to be creative about your job. Read *Life After Law*. It will change your life and the law."

—Alan M. Dershowitz, author of
Taking the Stand: My Life in the Law

" 'How do I get out of the law?' is a question that lawyers constantly ask me. Liz Brown's *Life After Law* answers that vital question. She gives practical information and timely advice—plus, real-life examples of lawyers who've made it to the other side. A worthwhile read for any lawyer who's thinking of making a career change."

—Vivia Chen, senior reporter at *The American Lawyer*
and the creator of *The Careerist* blog

"I'm a big believer in the power of serendipity, and *Life After Law* is an excellent guide for lawyers who are thinking about making a career change. The lawyers Liz Brown profiles are terrific examples of people who have taken their skills and education and applied them in new ways. Law and medicine are probably two of the most difficult professions to leave, and yet the skills and knowledge both require are broadly adaptable in other kinds of work. *Life After Law* is a must-read book for lawyers who dream of different careers."

—Jim Koch, brewer and founder
of Boston Beer Company

"If you've ever wondered what else you could do with a law degree, you will love *Life After Law*. Drawing from her own experience and the stories of thirty other inspiring ex-lawyers, Liz Brown has created an amazing toolkit for leaving the law and succeeding in a different career that capitalizes on your talents and fits your values. It's a fantastic read, and a resource you'll come back to over and over again."
—Gloria Feldt, co-founder and president of
Take The Lead and author of *No Excuses:*
9 Ways Women Can Change How We Think About Power

"*Life After Law* is not *just* a great book for lawyers, former lawyers, and law students considering non-traditional paths, but also a great reminder for all of us to 'follow our North Star' and carve our own path—a creative and meaningful one. This is not merely a 'think outside of the box' book, it is a 'leap outside of the box' dare."
—Peter H. Reynolds, author of *The Dot, Ish*, and
The North Star and founder of FableVision Studios

"Unhappy lawyers, this book is for you! Liz Brown's *Life After Law* is the definitive guide to alternate careers for lawyers, blending superb advice, strategy, and success stories in an authentic voice that could only come from someone who has been there herself."
—Carol Fishman Cohen, co-founder of iRelaunch
and co-author of *Back on the Career Track*

"*Life After Law* is an essential resource for any lawyer who questions staying in traditional practice. By telling the stories of actual ex-lawyers' transitions, and focusing on what made them successful, it provides an inspiring, realistic set of new career options and shows how versatile legal skills can be. No matter what you love to do, in or out of law practice, this book will show you a better way forward."
—Deborah Epstein Henry, Esq., founder & president,
Flex-Time Lawyers LLC; author of *Law and Reorder:*
Legal Industry Solutions for Restructure, Retention,
Promotion & Work/Life Balance

"This book is a powerful antidote for the tunnel vision often fostered by our legal culture and education. It thoughtfully reminds lawyers that they have acquired a wide range of knowledge and skills which they can use to improve both the world and their own lives."

—Michael Astrue, former
Commissioner of Social Security

"If you are a lawyer hoping that there is life beyond the law but fearing the impossibility of your yearning, this book is a must-read. Although there are many helpful books that instruct you to analyze your transferable skills and interests, here Liz Brown has filled a gaping hole in print resources: the stories of 30 lawyers who have successfully transferred their own skills into satisfying career paths outside the law. Bravo to Liz for providing such a compassionate and hopeful window into the possible future for so many unhappy lawyers who otherwise might fear to dream!"

—Ellen Ostrow, Ph.D. PCC,
Lawyers Life Coach LLC

"This is the *how to* book that women lawyers—heck, most lawyers—have been waiting for. Brown understands the bonds that tie so many attorneys to the profession that they and their families too often come to despise. She starts but doesn't stop with complaints that will be familiar to every J.D. in the land. Quickly covering the fools' gold of property, power, and prestige that has kept so many of us in platinum hand-cuffs, she lays out a step-by-step course of action that can take any lawyer from the courthouse or corporate conference room to a satisfying, productive and lucrative occupation. It takes courage, of course, but with Liz Brown by your side saying *you can do it!* you really can."

—Victoria Pynchon, J.D., LL.M, co-founder,
She Negotiates Consulting and Training

"Prepare to be uplifted! Liz Brown's *Life After Law* proves that lawyers can use their training to find non-traditional careers that leave them happy and fulfilled. With a refreshing candor and conversational style, this great book shows how smart lawyers are finding work they love outside of the corner office."

—Hollee Schwartz Temple, author of *Good Enough Is the New Perfect: Finding Happiness and Success in Modern Motherhood*

LIFE

after

LAW

LIFE === *after* === LAW

Finding Work You **LOVE** with the **J.D.** You **HAVE**

LIZ BROWN, J.D.

bibliomotion
books + media

First published by Bibliomotion, Inc.

33 Manchester Road
Brookline, MA 02446
Tel: 617-934-2427
www.bibliomotion.com

Printed in the United States of America

Library of Congress Cataloging-in-Publication Data

Brown, Liz.
    Life after law : finding work you love with the J.D. you have / Liz Brown.
        pages cm
    ISBN 978-1-937134-64-8 (pbk.) — ISBN 978-1-937134-65-5 (ebook) —
ISBN 978-1-937134-66-2 (en)
    1. Law—Vocational guidance—United States. I. Title.
    KF297.B725 2013
    340.023—dc23
                        2013020750

To the memory of Edward Eric Brown,
whose beautiful, too brief life taught me
never to take time for granted.

CONTENTS

Foreword by Gloria Cordes Larson, J.D.,
president of Bentley University   *XV*

Acknowledgments   *XIX*

Introduction   *XXI*

PART I   *The Depression Profession*   *1*

1 Why Are So Many Lawyers Unhappy?   *3*
2 The Bonds of Money, Status, and Purpose   *13*
3 Challenges and Alternatives for Women Lawyers   *21*

PART II   *Repurposing Your Law Career*   *33*

4 Reframing Your Preferred Skills   *35*
5 Where to Start When You Have No Idea
   Where to Start   *43*
6 How to Stop Worrying and Love the
   Informational Interview   *49*
7 Advocating for Your Next Career   *59*

PART III *The Role Models: Eight Basic Paths to
Career Happiness for Former Lawyers*   67

  8 The Writers   69

     Adam Liptak, *New York Times* Correspondent   70

     Kat Griffin, Founder and Editor-in-Chief,
     Corporette.com   74

     Elie Mystal, Editor, AbovetheLaw.com   78

     Stephanie Rowe, Fantasy and Romance
     Novelist   82

     Nathaniel Stearns, Art Advisor   86

  9 The Entrepreneurs   91

     Peter Dziedzic, Proprietor of skoah Boston   92

     Valerie Beck, Founder of Chicago
     Chocolate Walking Tours   96

     Christina Whelton, Founder of
     Place Boston   99

     Mary-Alice Brady, Founder of MosaicHub   103

 10 The Artisans   107

     Karina Gentinetta, Designer and Artist   108

     Zoe Mohler, Proprietor of Three Sisters
     Jewelry Design   112

     Warren Brown, Proprietor of CakeLove   116

 11 The Analysts   119

     Meredith Benedict, Health Care Strategist   120

     Sara Harnish, Non-Clinical Research Director   124

     Alison P. Ranney, Senior Recruiter   128

     Christopher Mirabile, Angel Group Leader   132

 12 The Professors   137

     Liz Gorman, Sociology Professor   138

Deb Volberg Pagnotta, Communications
    Professor   *141*

Katrina Lee, Clinical Law Professor   146

13 The Consultants   149

Greg Stone, Media Consultant   149

Susannah Baruch, Policy Consultant   153

Lisa Montanaro, Productivity Consultant   157

14 The Advocates   161

Eleanor Hoague, Immigrants' Rights Advocate   162

Deborah Felton, Executive Director of Senior
    Residence   166

Jen Atkins, Nurse   169

15 The Healers   173

Liz Mirabile, Health Coach   174

Clare Dalton, Acupuncturist   178

Van Lanckton, Rabbi   183

Will Meyerhofer, Psychotherapist   186

16 The Independent   191

Alan Rilla, Island Caretaker   192

Endnotes   197

References   199

FOREWORD

by Gloria Cordes Larson, J.D.,
president of Bentley University

1968 was a turning point for my generation. The assassinations of Dr. King and RFK threw a country already in turmoil over the Vietnam War into full-blown rebellion. More than 115 cities erupted in violence. Riots rocked the Democratic National Convention in Chicago. Black Power raised its proud fist at the Mexico City Olympics. And President Johnson spoke of a nation "challenged at home and abroad."

With that as a backdrop, I packed my bags and drove north from Virginia for my freshman year at Vassar College. I left early to participate in a retreat sponsored by Vassar and Yale. Led by our schools' chaplains, the group read books about race relations—*Malcolm X, Black Like Me, The Wretched of the Earth*, to name a few—and discussed their relationship to what was happening around us.

Like Paul on the road to Damascus, scales fell from my eyes. I was a socially committed student, perhaps a bit naïve, but these discussions in that environment cemented my desire to pursue justice by solving important public problems. I knew law school was in my future.

That sense of purpose and meaning has yet to fade, though nearly four decades have passed since I began my career setting up legal services for Virginia's elderly. I still wake up eager to solve problems like my childhood hero Nancy Drew, and I still seek to serve the greater good with integrity like my other idol,

Atticus Finch. But I no longer wake up as a practicing attorney in a law firm. I am a university president. And it's the toughest, most rewarding job of my career.

It also happens to be an excellent job for a lawyer, even though a recent survey by the *Chronicle of Higher Education* revealed that just 1 percent of college presidents hold law degrees. Consider the lawyer's tool kit: The legal mindset conditions you to dissect a problem through multiple lenses in pursuit of the right response. Lawyers are trained to negotiate, analyze, communicate, and lead effectively—invaluable assets in higher education, a noisy space of competing stakeholders and conflicting opinions.

I found my law school skill set to be equally valuable during other chapters of my career: As a federal government appointee focused on consumer protection; as the head of Boston's effort to build a new convention and exhibition center; and as a corporate board member in an era defined by regulatory and governance issues.

I did eventually spend time in a large law firm, helping lead a government relations practice. I was drawn to the job by a great public servant, the late U.S. Senator Paul Tsongas, who implored all of us to remember, "there must be a higher purpose to our journey." He inspired me to take a broad view of my legal training, even in the billable world of a big firm.

And that leads me to my larger point: Your law degree represents a bounty of skills, but those skills need to be teamed with passion and meaning and flexibility. At Bentley, we emphasize the need for college and graduate students to be prepared for unexpected opportunities. It's almost certain that they will change jobs, even careers, multiple times over the course of a lifetime. But the reality of fast-paced change isn't limited to the millennial generation; the "new normal" of our 21st century economy demands that mid-career professionals—including lawyers—remain open to applying their skills in completely different ways. I am living proof.

That's why *Life After Law* is such an important book. Now is the time to think broadly about your own aspirations and pay attention to what your internal voice is telling you. That's not something taught in American law schools, but it is critical to long-term career success. On top of that, every sector of society needs the talent and experience that many ex-lawyers offer. Getting there takes vision—imagination even— to see how you can use your strengths in different ways, and it takes the know-how to make the leap.

Life After Law is your guidebook. Written especially for lawyers and law students by an ex-law partner, it provides the specific guidance you need to find a career that is sustainable *and* rewarding.

Nobody is more qualified to write this book than Liz Brown. Liz is absolutely passionate about helping other lawyers find fulfilling work, especially outside of the law. She knows from her own experience how difficult it can be to leave the legal profession, especially without a clear idea of what to do next. She knows how challenging it can be to develop a network. She taught herself to do it. She understands the frustration of changing course more than once. And most important, Liz embodies the joy and fulfillment that comes with finding work that you're excited about and that capitalizes on the skills you love to use.

We hired Liz to teach at Bentley after she left a brilliant legal career. Having trained at Harvard Law School, she became a partner at one of the most prestigious intellectual property firms in the world. Then she did something too few lawyers have the courage to do: She walked away from her job when it no longer fit her priorities.

Although she started teaching as an adjunct, her talents and interest to do more became clear to everyone in short order. In fact, Liz is an incredibly gifted teacher. Her students offer high praise for the way she weaves her own experience as a litigator into the classroom. She emphasizes the practical application of law to the business world they are about to enter, using real examples, to help her students become savvier and more effective managers.

In *Life After Law*, Liz uses the same real-world approach to help lawyers and law students become savvier about leveraging their talents and skills. She echoes my old friend Nancy Drew in *The Hidden Staircase*, "I have a hunch from reading about old passageways that there may be one or more rooms off this tunnel." That's right, Nancy: There is more than one room—and one career—for lawyers. Thank you, Liz, for showing us the way!

ACKNOWLEDGMENTS

I wrote this book in order to help other people find joy in their work because so many people helped me in the same pursuit. When I first proposed the book, with Whitney Johnson's kind encouragement, I had no idea how rewarding or how challenging this experience would be. The process of researching and writing *Life After Law*, while working two part-time jobs, competing over six months for my dream job, and mothering a young child, was only feasible because the following people were so generous. I am deeply grateful to all of them.

To David: your constant support and unjustified faith allowed me to change careers, write this book, and do several other things I used to consider impossible. Thank you for finding me, for challenging my prejudices, and for loving me for who I am instead of what I had done.

To Mom, Dad and D.J.: I can never thank you enough for raising me with such boundless love, encouragement, and joy. Everything I'm proud of being and doing stems from what you taught me. Thank you for my education, formal and informal, and for the freedom to chart my own course.

To my wonderful friends around the world: I would never have gotten through law school, law practice, my career drift, the early stages of motherhood, and the later stages of book writing without you. A special burst of gratitude to Phoebe Peabody, whose friendship has meant so much to me since I started my own transition.

To all of my mentors, sponsors, and teachers, including everyone who took the time to talk with me about his or her own career path when I was figuring out mine: thank you for honoring me with your generosity and wisdom. Carol Fishman Cohen, Marianne DelPo Kulow, Robert Bird, and Tanya Holton were especially kind. I am grateful for every single conversation, and I will continue to pay it forward.

To each of the courageous ex-lawyers profiled in *Life After Law*: thank you for sharing your knowledge and experiences with me for this book. Your stories are invaluable. It isn't easy to talk about moments of doubt, let alone months or years of it. I know the transition isn't over for many of you, and I look forward to seeing what you do next.

To my friends, students, and colleagues at Bentley University: thank you for welcoming me so warmly into a new professional home. It is an honor and an inspiration to work with you.

And most of all, to Rachel: you are the central joy of my life. I couldn't be more proud of you or more grateful to be your mother. I love you more than everything else put together.

INTRODUCTION

In writing a book about alternative careers for lawyers, I know that I risk offending lawyers who are happy in traditional practice. Many lawyers genuinely like their work. I have worked alongside lawyers who are good at their jobs, fulfilled by their jobs, and happy with their lives overall. There are happy lawyers in every area of the law and every type of practice. I have the greatest respect for these lawyers. This book is not for them.

This book is for the other lawyers, the ones who get that gnawing feeling in their stomachs as they approach the office every day and as they check their e-mail at night. It is for the lawyers who feel trapped by their work rather than energized by it. These lawyers are not sure how they got to this point or what they can realistically do about it. They can't figure out how to change professions without losing status, increasing debt, disappointing loved ones, and/or uprooting the sense of self they have been building, as lawyers, for years.

I've been on both sides of this divide. For several years after law school, I enjoyed being a litigator. And then I became more miserable litigating than I could admit even to myself. Even now, I'm not sure when the cracks started to appear because I was so good at quashing those feelings and keeping my focus on work.

Everything looked good from the outside. I progressed up the associate ranks and eventually made partner. But I hated fighting all day and checking my e-mail every waking minute, both serious problems for a litigator. I decided to leave my law firm when my daughter was born. I had no idea what I would do next. It was like jumping off a professional cliff.

Since leaving full-time law practice, I've been the executive director of an angel investor network and a business law professor. I now teach full time, and I love my work. The combination of lecturing and writing suits my personality, which teeters on the border between extrovert and introvert. I've kept the parts of legal work that I most enjoyed—writing, oral advocacy, and working with a range of interesting people—and left behind the billable hours, the constant availability to clients, and the verbal combat, all of which I'm happier without.

I've also had the privilege of mentoring many lawyers who want to leave the law but aren't sure where to start. Many have worked so hard on projects they don't enjoy that they no longer recognize what they do like. The stress that comes from channeling so much energy into something that doesn't reflect who they are or what they value eventually becomes unbearable.

This book dispels the myths lawyers circulate among themselves that leaving the law is unrealistic, unprofitable, and/or only for failures. It is none of these things. Changing careers is, certainly, hard—much harder than it was for most lawyers to get their first legal job after law school. It also requires a level of self-analysis that most people have never been asked to do.

This book offers lawyers a framework for identifying and moving into alternative careers. It challenges the notion that starting over means starting from zero. If you reframe the skills and strengths you have enjoyed using and the passions you may have put aside, it is not only possible but likely that you will succeed in an entirely different arena, no matter when you graduated from law school.

Because role models are invaluable, *Life After Law* also tells the stories of thirty former lawyers who have gone on to a variety of other careers. Some changed course in their twenties, after their first or second year of practice. Others started new careers in their fifties, after thirty or more years in law. Many took time off before they started a new venture. The amount of time they took ranges from a few months to eighteen years. Some left government roles, and others came from private practice or nonprofits. A few moved directly into a profession they loved, but most tried a few different things before figuring out or just landing in what truly made them happy.

None of them regrets leaving the law. Not all of them disliked law, in fact, but they all moved on to new careers that are far more satisfying to them than legal work was. In fact, to this day, I have not met a single former lawyer who regrets changing professions. Most wish they had done it sooner.

My confidence that any lawyer can find work she loves through a combination of introspection, research, creativity, and persistence stems from my own experience doing just that. Ten years ago, I would never have thought of leaving the law. I liked being a litigator. I felt lucky to have a job that paid me well to do things I was good at, like writing, arguing, and organizing information. If career satisfaction meant being content with my career, I had it. I never thought of wanting more.

My family, while exceptionally loving, set a low bar for career satisfaction. My parents had a "that's why they call it work" approach to their jobs. My father's group insurance sales position played a distant second to Freemasonry in terms of personal fulfillment (not that he would ever use that phrase). My mother stayed at home with her three children until the youngest was in elementary school, and then she got a part-time job that made her miserable. She complained often about how her bosses and colleagues treated her, about how they belittled her intelligence and ridiculed her plans to finish her college degree. She earned her degree from Harvard at the age of fifty-five and left her job the following month. As a result, I grew up assuming that it was at least common, if not normal, to hate your job.

I put off my own career decision until one was more or less made for me. As an undergraduate, I wanted to study everything: anthropology, literature, art history, and social studies. The History and Literature concentration offered me the chance to major in books, on the condition that I would write a senior thesis. Being squirreled away in the library carrels, researching the porch in antebellum Southern women's literature and blissfully disconnected from any kind of preprofessional training, was nirvana.

I thought about academia, but after four years in the Ivy League, the last thing I wanted to do was lock myself up in another ivory tower. Instead, I lined up a job working for a small consulting firm that helped companies develop work–family balance initiatives and early childhood education. After two years of work supporting the principals, yet failing to accomplish anything independently, I was ready to go back to the comfort zone of school.

At the time, I knew nothing about business school. I had no idea what people with MBAs did, but I sensed that they didn't get to read or write much, and I wasn't going to sign up for that.

When I applied to law school, I thought I might keep working on family policy issues, with the greater credibility a law degree confers, but I wasn't sure. Law school was a socially acceptable way to defer a more detailed career decision that I lacked the self-knowledge to make. Lacking a lodestar, I wanted to keep my options as wide open as possible. I put in applications to several law schools, and then backpacked alone around Central America for a few months, calling my parents every week or two for a postal update. In a Guatemalan bar, I learned that I'd gotten into Harvard Law School.

I didn't fully understand the magnitude of law firm salaries until the second or third week of law school, when on-campus recruiting kicked in. Almost sure I would never want to work for a big firm, but mindful of my tuition payments, I applied for a summer associate job. It couldn't hurt, I reasoned, to see what working in one of those firms was like before rejecting the most lucrative career path outright. My parents were more impressed by the summer law firm gig than by law school itself. They had sacrificed for almost twenty years for their children's education, and this gave them a result to brag about.

That summer, I worked on pro bono copyright cases and volunteered at a legal clinic. There was no limit to the amount of good I could do from the firm's plush offices, I thought. I went out to lunch with senior lawyers at sparkling restaurants nestled inside five-star hotels. I went on cruises in Boston Harbor and to brunch at the partners' sprawling estates. The lawyers I met were bright and personable. I couldn't wait to interview with another firm for the following year. Believing that I would enjoy being a lawyer helped me make it through the misery of law school.

I spent my second summer at a large law firm in San Francisco, earning a full-time offer. After I had accepted it and, while I was bartending on campus, I met the partner who was recruiting on campus for Allen & Overy's London office. That conversation led to an interview, a callback, and a glorious year at the only law firm I have ever worked for that had its own pub. But I wanted to litigate, so I headed back to the United States and stayed at big firms for eleven more years.

My career path was not even vaguely creative. I was a litigator near Silicon Valley in the late 1990s, so I handled intellectual property cases almost by default. When I was unhappy with my job, I told myself that a different law firm was all the change I needed. In fact, it was the only change I could imagine, other than working for the government. It never occurred to me that the problem might be private practice, or law itself.

At least, that's what I recall. Friends tell me that I muttered now and then about leaving the profession, but I don't remember keeping that thought in my head for long. Instead, I moved from one enormous law firm to another, billing a few thousand hours each year. As a senior associate, I landed one of the nicest offices I have ever seen, on the thirty-second floor in a downtown San Francisco high-rise, with sliding glass doors leading to a large patio. Hummingbirds would regularly buzz around the potted bottlebrush trees, distracting me during conference calls.

I was engaged to a nice guy, until he broke things off six weeks before the wedding. He let me know by phone, since I was usually at the office. The idea that certain important things were beyond my control, and couldn't be corralled through logic or hard work, was a new and extremely unpleasant concept. One thing within my control was taking care of my health. I started taking yoga classes near the office.

Yoga, it turns out, can be fatal to denial. It forced me to slow down, breathe deeply, and quiet my mind. Let me explain how terrifying that was. I don't know whether I had ever been centered before practicing yoga. The word "centered" made me snicker. Once I started breathing deeply, I realized that the fight had gone out of me. As a senior associate, I spent most of my time choreographing litigation and strategizing about how to take down opposing counsel. I didn't want to oppose counsel anymore. I wanted to collaborate, as I had in the pro bono cases I was doing less and less of.

Yoga was changing me, but it could only do so much. I still couldn't face the idea of giving up law entirely. How would I make money? What else was I qualified to do? I was getting close to partnership, and starting again at the bottom of another pyramid was unthinkable. When would I even have time to think about this, given my billable minimum? I knew only that I wanted to be near my family, especially when my father's health started to fail. My parents were still in Boston so I moved back, and put the whole idea of career change on hold.

My San Francisco firm did not have a Boston office, so I moved to a new firm. A few days after accepting the Boston firm's offer, I updated the hometown on my Match.com profile and almost immediately met the man I would marry the following year. In my new firm, I started as counsel and was voted into the partnership six months later.

Making partner did nothing to quell the dissatisfaction I had started to feel in San Francisco, but it did make it easier to think about leaving. I no longer had to worry that my departure would be taken as a sign that I wasn't qualified to make partner. I had nothing more to prove, to myself or anyone else. Becoming pregnant with my daughter forced the issue. My concerns about practicing law grew exponentially when I compared work to being with my child. Once I held her, there wasn't even a question in my mind as to what I should do. The pull to be with my daughter was more powerful than anything I had felt before, in any context.

I did consider, briefly, the issue of role models. I would have been the only female litigation partner in my firm's Boston office with a small child. By leaving, I lost the ability to mentor female associates and to show by example that you can have a thriving law practice and a happy family life. But to do so, I would have had to delegate parenting, the best part of my life so far. I wasn't willing to give up that experience, especially when I might never have it again. I might also have had to lie. I didn't believe that I, personally, could have it all, and I didn't want to suggest otherwise to anyone else. I also considered whether I would be doing my child a disservice by walking away from so much money. Leaving the firm with no replacement income on the horizon was an enormous financial hit. But I had grown up in a low-income, high-affection family, and I knew that a happy childhood did not depend on an excess of material goods.

After the hormones wore off and the impact of my decision became clearer, I began to think about next steps. Even figuring out how to approach the issue was daunting. Should I choose a new job that was just a job, or should I aim higher? Should I prioritize form, including location and benefits, over substance?

Should I give up law entirely? It seemed vaguely unwise, given all the money and time I had spent on becoming a lawyer, but I felt so relieved to have left private practice that the idea of going back was intolerable. Besides that, I was tired of thinking hard, and working at Whole Foods sounded kind of good. Should I automatically exclude any job that might require additional schooling? I couldn't imagine taking classes again, or adding debt to lack of income.

I thought I should at least try to find something I'd enjoy, and that I had a reasonable chance of being good at. Even with that decision made, I had no idea where to start.

It was embarrassing to admit that I didn't know much about other jobs. I flipped with interest through my daughter's Richard Scarry book, *What Do People Do All Day?* I forced myself to ask for informational interviews, and learned how to do so effectively. When someone's work sounded interesting to me, I asked her out for coffee.

The kindness of strangers amazed me. I had no idea how generous people were until I got out of law firms. I had informational interviews at the Museum of Fine Arts, one of my favorite places, and learned that my intellectual property experience wouldn't count for much there. Recruiters, marketers, psychologists, and food writers all sat down with me to talk about their work.

I thought about going into development, although I called it fundraising until someone corrected me. I learned about different niches within development, and started going to professional association meetings. I enrolled in a Fundraising Basics course, both to demonstrate genuine interest and to do more due diligence. Many people recommended planned giving because it involves trusts and estates law, with some tax thrown in. I knew nothing about those areas and didn't particularly want to learn.

I talked myself into focusing on donor relations instead, thinking that it would allow me to use the writing, analytical, and interpersonal skills I had enjoyed in litigation in a less adversarial setting. I parlayed my experience counseling clients into an aptitude for working with high-net-worth individuals. I narrowed my search to secondary schools. As I talked with more people who had the job I thought I wanted, I realized I didn't want it after all. It was embarrassing to go back to the drawing board, but better than committing to another unfulfilling job.

At that point, I decided that some external structure might help. Bentley University was running a seminar for mothers who had taken time off. I signed up with a friend. Getting outside perspective on what else I could do with my skills was invaluable, but it didn't lead directly to my next job.

It did, however, lead to a conversation with Marianne Kulow, the business law professor who was facilitating the seminar. She suggested that I think about teaching law to business students, which I had not known was a possibility. She offered to set up an informational interview with the chair of her department at Bentley University. I left that interview with an unexpected offer to teach one course as an adjunct. Neither the department chair nor I knew whether I could teach well, or how I would like teaching, since I had never done it before. But it was a short-term commitment for both of us, and I jumped at the chance.

For my first class, I had an established syllabus to work from, with standard reading assignments. That first class led to other teaching opportunities, each a bit more complex and flexible in how I might present and test the material. Those classes went well enough that I was asked to design a new course for Bentley's MBA program. Teaching could be a wonderful second career, I thought, if someone would pay me to do it full time.

I should point out that I made virtually no money teaching those courses. It was, for all purposes, a barely paid internship, and I made the most of it. I threw myself into every extracurricular activity that might help me make connections. I volunteered to organize the regional conference of the Academy of Legal Studies in Business. One of the first people I met at my first conference is still one of my most valued mentors. I wrote papers and presented research that wasn't required of me as an adjunct.

At the same time, the lack of income was starting to wear on us. As kind as my husband was about it, I hated being financially dependent. I refocused my attention on earning at least enough to cover the cost of day care.

One of the things I had most enjoyed while practicing law was organizing women's networks. I was good at managing groups of people, and I am passionate about women in business. I started working that into my informational interviews. When one of my networking contacts told me that Golden Seeds, a network of angel investors who fund women-led, high-growth companies, was hiring a part-time executive director, it seemed like the perfect opportunity. I worked with Golden Seeds for more than a year, until my dream job opened up a few miles away.

When a rare full-time, tenure-track position opened up in Bentley's law department, my colleagues knew I could teach well and I knew I would enjoy teaching there. My demonstrated success and confidence, together with the extra papers and presentations I had worked on over the previous three years, gave me the edge I needed when the school conducted a nationwide search. I was thrilled to get the position.

My story illustrates the following tenets of alternative career searches for lawyers:

1. **You don't need to know where you are going to end up at the right place.** When I started my search, I cast a wide net for potential new jobs. I asked for a lot of interviews. Then I headed for development. I spent a year managing an angel network before deciding to switch into academia full time. Every step led me to the next one, but I couldn't see the whole path at any point in the process.

2. **It is never too late to become who you might have been.** As a college student, I loved research and writing but rejected the idea of going into academia because I thought it was too disen-

gaged from the real world. When I circled back to academia, I tapped into the love of learning that had gotten lost in my law practice. Many of the people profiled in this book built second careers around things that they had always enjoyed, but which didn't lead to promising career choices earlier in their lives. Working with what you love can be a powerful driver of success.

3. Networking and internships can work wonders. If it hadn't been for my conversation with Marianne Kulow, I would never have known that you can teach business law outside of law schools. Once I realized how much I enjoyed teaching, and how few full-time jobs teaching business law existed, I did everything I could to make myself a good candidate for the tenure-track position that I knew would open up sooner or later. I had always worked hard, and I channeled my extra work energy into research, writing, and presenting. When my dream job opened up, I was as ready for the intense competition as I could have possibly been.

4. You can use your skills to do any number of things, as long as you can talk other people into it. As part 2 of this book explains, what you've enjoyed doing in the past can be the starting point for an entirely different career. I thought that my experience counseling clients might lead to a successful career in development. My experience organizing networks of women lawyers helped me qualify for a job organizing networks of largely female angel investors. My love of talking in courtrooms translated to a love of teaching in classrooms. But I had to reframe those skills and make those connections before I could convince anyone else to do so. If I can do it, you can too.

PART I

The Depression Profession

There are a lot of unhappy lawyers out there. In one study, 52 percent of lawyers reported being dissatisfied at work. That is probably not because of their income. Law remains one of the best-paying professions, although the statistics are skewed by what the largest firms pay.

Money is not buying lawyers happiness. In fact, lawyers are far more likely to be depressed than other people. One study reports that about 20 percent of lawyers suffer from clinical depression, twice the national average. According to Martin Seligman, the founder of positive psychology, law is a troubled field:

> Researchers at John Hopkins University found statistically significant elevations of major depressive disorder in only three of 104 occupations surveyed. When adjusted for socio-demographics, lawyers topped the list, suffering from depression at a rate of 3.6 times higher than employed persons generally. Lawyers also suffer from alcoholism and illegal drug use at rates far higher than nonlawyers. The divorce rate among lawyers, especially women, also appears to be higher than the divorce rate among other professionals.[1]

Law may be the only profession with a sub-profession dedicated to helping people get out of it. It is easy to find consultants who specialize in counseling former lawyers and blogs devoted to the needs of depressed lawyers. Many psychotherapists treat only lawyers.

Lawyers themselves don't find these statistics surprising. Karina Gentinetta, a former lawyer who became an artist and designer, often talked with the other partners at her former firm about getting out. The sadness she saw in many of the other partners' lives took different forms, including divorce, kids with drug problems, and alcoholism. "They had all the money in the world, and they were miserable," she says. None of them knew what they would do if they didn't practice law.

Lawyers are unhappy for many reasons. While every dissatisfied lawyer has a unique set of concerns, certain factors come into play more than others. The next chapter examines some of the most pervasive and troubling issues lawyers face today.

1

WHY ARE SO MANY LAWYERS UNHAPPY?

One reason so many lawyers are unhappy is that it is easy to go to law school for the wrong reasons. Getting a J.D. is so expensive, and the law profession so insular, that walking away when they realize that law practice is not (or no longer) right for them can feel like an impossibility. Another reason for lawyers' dissatisfaction is that the legal profession has changed. It is more intensely competitive and less stable than ever before.

BECOMING LAWYERS BY DEFAULT

Much of the problem lies in the way people become lawyers in the first place. Young people who like to argue and/or write may choose law school without really knowing what lawyers do, how they do it, or whether their personalities and interests fit well into any niche within the legal profession. Many college graduates choose law school in part because they think it will open up a wide range of lucrative and/or world-saving job options, allowing them to defer more specific career planning for a few more years. Once they get into school, and into debt, their range of choices can look much narrower.

The law school assumption for liberal arts majors is part of a larger problem. As a society, we funnel smart, ambitious people into a limited number of professional tracks. If they like logic and language, or if they are just good debaters, we encourage them to go to law school. If they excel at science, we suggest medical school. If they're business oriented, or they like numbers, we push business school brochures in their direction. Conversely, there is little cultural support for a smart kid who loves to read but wants to fix motorcycles for a living or for a microbiology whiz who wants to become an animator.

Young people often choose careers based on insufficient information about their own strengths and skills. As a professor, I often meet bright students who know little about who they are and therefore what kinds of work might be most fulfilling. Many students' career choices are shaped by external forces such as:

- Notions of what people with similar talents tend to do
- Imperatives from family members who help finance their education
- Attenuated interactions with professionals during high school and college
- Romanticized views of professions based on media depictions of them
- The simple goal of wealth maximization

What's missing from this list is a sense of self-knowledge that is admittedly hard to form. People who have not yet had much professional experience beyond retail or service jobs may know little about their talents. Even those who have taken personality tests like the Myers-Briggs Type Indicator assessment or career assessments like Skill Scan have limited experience using the skills these tests detect.

For lawyers, making this professional choice early has especially long-lasting effects. A recent college graduate who goes into marketing can change direction relatively early and easily.

Recent law school graduates find it much harder to change direction for financial reasons alone. The amount of law school debt law students incur, often on the order of $250,000, can seem to limit their career options. A law student may find a public service job appealing, for example, but it may be unrealistic in light of her loan obligations.

To some extent, the fact that postgraduate options appear limited is an inherited problem. We are not so far removed from a generation whose career choices were narrower than ours. Many lawyers were raised by parents whose careers were informed more by class, education, and geography than by personal interest. Geographic and socioeconomic immobility limited their choices. The question of what they should do with their lives was one to be answered pragmatically, not soulfully.

As a consequence, many parents did not encourage broad career exploration for their kids—at least, not in practice. As Valerie Beck, founder of Chicago Chocolate Walking Tours, recalls, "I was brought up to believe that I could do anything. But 'anything' had an asterisk after it, because by 'anything' my parents really meant 'doctor or lawyer.'" They wanted their children to have a better life, but "better" often meant "better paid" rather than "better fitting."

SLIDING FROM SCHOOL TO PRACTICE

Just as going to law school doesn't require much self-knowledge, choosing a first job or two after law school is often a no-brainer in the best and worst senses. Few law schools do a great job of encouraging students to look beyond private practice, in part because career services offices tend to be overtaxed. Law students looking into other career options can feel like they are doing something wrong, or conceding defeat. Corporate employers, for their part, aren't always receptive to the idea that law students can succeed in nonlegal roles.

While it is increasingly difficult for any law school graduate to get a job, the easiest path for many is to join a firm. Many law schools mainstream graduates into large law firms, with summer associate programs designed to provide an easy transition from school to work. Will Meyerhofer, a former attorney who became a therapist, compares his transition from New York University School of Law to his first job at Sullivan & Cromwell to a ride at Disney World. "The school set up the interviews, and they spoon-fed us what we needed to know, and then we got our offers," he says. He didn't need to put a lot of thought into it. It was an exhilarating ride, until it ended.

Yet large law firms, with their pyramid structure, are designed for attrition. A small number of equity partners rely on a larger number of nonequity partners and counsel to manage their cases. Most of the lawyers in larger firms are associates, the worker bees whose research, writing, deposing, and court appearances keep everything running. There isn't room for all of them in the partnership. During their annual review, some number of associates will be counseled out every year. Some will leave by choice. Increasingly, associates are vulnerable to group layoffs that have little to do with their merit. Whether the associates leave voluntarily or not, the fact is that many of them simply have to go.

Even lawyers who remain in private practice may feel that they didn't make the right choice. Indeed, it's easy for them to feel like they made no choice at all. Most competent lawyers have a history of accomplishment, and law firms define accomplishment narrowly (e.g., making partner or counsel). Once a lawyer has made partner, he finds himself at the bottom of another pyramid: this time, a pyramid of partners. It's often said that making partner is like a pie-eating contest where the prize is more pie. It is easy to see why so many of these attorneys feel disillusioned and dissatisfied with their careers.

Many associates find partnership itself unappealing, if measured by any standard other than income. After a few years, most associates have had a chance to see how partners live in some detail. Partners work long hours, often at the expense of close family relationships and sometimes at the expense of their health. Several former associates told me that seeing what it was like to be a partner in more detail made them realize that it wasn't the life they wanted. That leaves them with the question of what to do next, since the profession doesn't provide any easy answers. The traditional alternative of going in-house is increasingly difficult, and doesn't guarantee a shorter workday.

Unhappiness in the profession is by no means limited to large law firms. The bases for lawyers' disenchantment with the law are as varied as the lawyers themselves. There are deeply dissatisfied lawyers in smaller firms, working just as hard as lawyers in larger firms, and in equally stressful conditions, for much less pay. Professional dissatisfaction takes root in public defenders' offices, in nonprofits, in corporate general counsel's offices, and in every other kind of practice. The bureaucracy and pay grade limitations of government work can be particularly frustrating over time, often outweighing the benefits of a more predictable schedule.

THE BROKEN PROMISE OF STABILITY

Many lawyers went into the profession assuming that they would always be able to find satisfying, well-paid work. In fact, the legal profession has never been less stable. Firms are downsizing and shedding associates in ways that were practically unheard of in the past few decades. Making partner is increasingly difficult, and fewer associates aspire to it for a variety of reasons. While many lawyers understand this shift in the profession, other people still perceive law as a stable profession.

Twenty years ago, the legal world looked different. Law firms essentially promised associates that their talent and hard work would be rewarded with partnership someday. Partners had job security, financial stability, and a team of junior lawyers at their beck and call. Summer associate programs previewed the good life, and associates were seldom fired except for cause. The lock-step raises that big firms still offer associates as they progress from year to year supported this relatively stable image.

Even ten years ago, it would have been hard to predict the dramatic changes the legal profession has gone through. Large firms imploded and merged in unprecedented numbers. Heller Ehrman, a Top 20 law firm in 2005, declared bankruptcy in 2008, leaving hundreds of lawyers and staff people without a job during the worst recession in decades. Thelen Reid collapsed in 2009, followed by Howrey & Simon in 2011. Dewey & LeBoeuf closed its doors in 2012, and other firms are likely to follow.

At the surviving firms, things are not much better. Hiring dropped as law school graduation rates increased. *The New York Times* noted that only 55 percent of law school graduates in 2011 had a law-related job nine months after graduation.[1] Twenty-eight percent of graduates were unemployed or underemployed. At the twenty law schools with the best employment track records, only 83 percent of graduates were working as lawyers. Only 31 percent of graduates of the bottom twenty schools were practicing law.

Law school graduates who do get job offers have less security than ever before. Many of the largest firms have deferred incoming associates and radically cut back on their summer programs. Waves of associate layoffs have led to increased competitiveness within firms, and collegiality has decreased. Even partners, who used to have informal tenure at their firms, are being culled or de-equitized, which was unthinkable ten years ago. More than half of the managing partners and firm chairs who responded to an *American Lawyer* survey said that they planned to let between one and five partners go in the coming year.[2]

College students are starting to realize that a J.D. doesn't represent the same kind of job security it used to. The number of people applying to law school is dropping, according to the American Bar Association. In 2012, eight thousand fewer students enrolled in law school than in 2010, when the number of entering students hit an all-time high. That represents a 15 percent decline in just two years, and a 9 percent decline since 2011.[3]

GIVING UP THE FIGHT

Another reason so many lawyers, and litigators in particular, are unhappy is that they get tired of fighting for a living. Many new lawyers find the adversarial nature of litigation thrilling. For someone who has always been good at arguing, getting professional credit for that skill can be a heady experience.

Spending day after day in a dogfight, even an intellectually challenging one, can also be draining. It can be hard on families, a problem that may become more urgent as time goes on and other pressures build. Over time, many lawyers question the effectiveness of litigation compared with negotiation, collaboration, and other means of conflict resolution that traditional law practice tends to discount. The field of collaborative law, while immensely attractive to many people, remains so small that it can barely absorb all of the lawyers who want to go into it. Collaborative family lawyers, who supplant the traditionally adversary divorce process with mediation-based practices, are relatively few in number.

For some people, shifting from traditional law practice to a consulting role is the best way to sidestep an overtly competitive environment. Susannah Baruch, a public policy advisor in Washington, D.C., started her practice on Capitol Hill. She had always enjoyed working on policy, especially reproductive rights issues, but didn't like the "sharp elbows" culture of lawmaking. By pursuing a career in public policy consulting, she was able to put her analytical skills to use for matters she cares about in a more collaborative way. Her consulting role also allowed her more flexibility while her children were young.

For other people, leaving law entirely is the best way to have a more constructive career. Peter Dziedzic, a former private equity lawyer who was compelled to work on bankruptcy cases, left law in part because he no longer wanted to spend his days dismantling companies. As the owner of one of Boston's most successful spas, his workdays are much more rewarding now (albeit no shorter).

THE PERVASIVE EFFECTS OF UNHAPPINESS

Many lawyers are unhappy because they work with and for other unhappy people. What happens to a decent person who is forced to work long hours at a job she doesn't like, under conditions she can't control, for clients who don't express appreciation or even acknowledge her existence? When people work under these conditions, with little time for personal life and even less time for the outside interests they used to have, they may become bitter, vindictive, or passive-aggressive. They are not fun to work with. They are not fun to be.

People skills are not as valued within firms as one might hope. When hardworking and high-billing associates come up for partnership, their work is evaluated primarily on how well they meet client needs. How well they work with junior lawyers, in contrast, rarely factors into the analysis. At many firms, the treatment of secretaries and paralegals matters more than the treatment of junior lawyers. The idea of 360-degree reviews is far less common in law firms than in their clients' corporations, especially where rainmakers are concerned.

Of course, many senior lawyers are genuinely interested in mentoring associates, increasing diversity, and helping junior associates become better lawyers. Some partners also walk the talk of promoting pro bono work. Jack Londen, a senior partner at Morrison & Foerster, for example, dedicates significant time every year to public service and to mentoring associates. I had the good fortune to work with Jack early in my career, and it made me feel better about my own habit of maxing out my pro bono hours year to year. Unfortunately, leaders like Jack are exceptional.

Another ill effect of law practice is that it leaves little room for the other passions that make people engaging to work with. Many large law firms recruit candidates based not only on their academic performance but also on their extracurricular interests. Ironically, these firms' billable hour requirements make it virtually impossible for associates to keep up with the interests that made them such attractive candidates in the first place. The demands of practice have the unfortunate effect of flattening people out, and interesting people generally don't want to get flattened.

Some lawyers carve out more time for their passions by changing practice areas before leaving law altogether. Bob Blumenthal, now a Grammy-winning jazz critic, found that he no longer had time for jazz when he joined a private firm after law school. Although he had some evenings free, his schedule was too unpredictable to commit to concert tickets on a regular basis. By switching to government work, he was able to write more jazz reviews on the side. Some of those reviews appeared in *Rolling Stone* and *The Atlantic*. Eventually, he was able to leave his government job and write full time. After six years, he was earning twice as much as a jazz critic as he had while practicing law, and his income continued to climb from there.

Many more lawyers, however, just remain unhappy. Many went to law school with a limited understanding of who they are, what lawyers actually do, and whether they would enjoy practicing law. Others found that law wasn't what they expected or grew to dislike it over time. Many worked long hours with colleagues who became less kind and less interesting as time went on, or were perhaps just unpleasant to begin with.

If so many lawyers are unhappy, why don't more of them leave? Lawyers stay in unsatisfying jobs for a few powerful reasons. We'll examine these in detail in the next chapter.

2

THE BONDS OF MONEY, STATUS, AND PURPOSE

Leaving a legal career remains one of the most difficult things many lawyers can envision, no matter how unhappy they are. It means giving up the professional identity they have invested their time and money in. It may mean going without a professional identity for a time as they explore alternatives. It means giving up the status that law practice conveys and the relatively easy access to high salaries they may have become dependent on. Lawyers are notoriously risk-averse and accomplishment-oriented on the whole, which doesn't help matters. For every lawyer who musters the courage and vision to change his job, hundreds more would make that change if they knew how to overcome these obstacles.

When unhappy lawyers think about changing careers, their keen analytical minds produce so many objections that it can be hard to keep track of them all. By far, the most common are the threatened loss of status and money. At a deeper level, however, it can be hard to picture viable alternatives. Many lawyers cannot see themselves as anything other than lawyers.

It can also be hard to walk away from the goal of pursuing justice. Many people become lawyers because they want to "do good while doing well." At first glance, it may seem like leaving the law means abandoning that principle. As we'll see, many ex-lawyers find ways to heal the world outside the practice of law.

THE GOLDEN HANDCUFFS

The first concern most lawyers have about leaving law is money. Recent law school graduates can emerge with $250,000 or more in debt. Working in a private practice firm is the most obvious way to pay down that debt. The pipeline from law school to private practice makes the transition fairly easy. In the fall of 2012, the starting salaries of large law firms averaged around $160,000, making them among the most lucrative entry-level jobs in the country. In New York, some firms were paying first year associates $160,000 *in bonuses alone.*

These salaries would be tempting to anyone, regardless of her debt load. After years of student living, it feels good to have a nice apartment and some five-star dining experiences, even if you only have time for takeout because you have a big research memo due in the morning.

Getting used to that income is all too easy, and it only gets harder to leave the money behind as time passes. By the time school debt comes under control, many lawyers have taken on significant mortgages, enrolled their kids in private schools that cost as much as college, and/or engaged a nanny. Giving up any of these expenses, and negotiating that sacrifice with a spouse, can be as daunting as living with longer-term debt.

Debt, of course, is only one side of this coin. Even after the major educational debts have been paid off, and the mortgages at least mitigated, it can be hard to give up the relatively comfortable lifestyle that large salaries make possible. Unlike many other people who dislike their jobs, unhappy lawyers can often afford to treat themselves well. One way to make an otherwise unhappy life bearable is to buy nice things. You may not be able to control your case schedule, but you can make yourself feel better with a nice car, an upscale vacation, or a Louis Vuitton

Speedy. But this kind of self-soothing only goes so far. As one ex-lawyer told me, "My law firm colleagues tended to surround themselves with things. I wanted to surround myself with relationships and experiences."

Other expenses come with the job. The culture of high-status professionals, including lawyers, makes some lifestyle costs necessary. Women lawyers, in particular, may end up spending more on their wardrobes than other women because their jobs informally demand it.

Most ex-lawyers find their way over time to making a comfortable salary. Although most people earn less when they leave private practice, some ex-lawyers find that they earn even more when they succeed in a new field. There are short-term savings too. Many job-related expenses, like suits, may go away with the transition to a new field. More importantly, these ex-lawyers' lives become more comfortable, even when they live in smaller houses.

STAYING IMPRESSIVE

The social status of being a lawyer, especially in a firm, can be even harder to leave than the money. In an era of ever-decreasing attention spans, the ability to impress someone by mentioning your title, your office location, or your firm can feel irreplaceable. It's a lot easier to answer the question, "So, what do you do?" with "I'm a patent lawyer" than with "Well, I used to practice law, but now I'm looking into my next thing" or "I'm a barista." Law is still a generally respected profession, lawyer jokes notwithstanding.

The long, expensive training necessary to practice law also creates a sense of group identity that can be hard to replace. Many lawyers find a collegiality in their bar associations that exists in few other fields. Saying "I'm a lawyer" asserts membership in an elite club, one that inherently equates work and self.

For people who grew up in lower-income homes, ceding status

can be especially difficult. They may be the first in their family to go to graduate school or to make a six-figure salary. Moving up the socioeconomic ladder is an accomplishment in itself. Giving up the status of law can appear to undo that accomplishment. These lawyers may fear letting down the people whose support helped them succeed in the first place. Peter Dziedzic, the ex-lawyer who owns one of Boston's top-rated spas, found that his émigré parents were unsure about his career change at first. "I was the first person in my family to go to college," he points out, "and it was much easier for them to get excited about my going to Yale than about my starting this business."

Loss of status can be especially hard for lawyers in private practice who haven't yet made partner. As they pass the fifth-year associate mark, the question creeps up: Will people think I am leaving because I'm not good enough? The assumption that all good associates will make partner is, of course flawed, yet it's still prevalent. Nobody wants to give friends, family, or future employers the impression that he just couldn't cut it. In addition, most nonlawyers underestimate what it takes to make it to the senior associate ranks to begin with: the interminable hours, the "rush" projects that senior partners still had not looked at several days after the projects were due, and so on. Becoming a senior associate represents a serious investment of time.

The loss of status associated with leaving law is often only temporary. Many former lawyers go on to more impressive careers because their new careers make better use of their skills and passions. Adam Liptak, for example, is the national Supreme Court correspondent for the *New York Times*. Warren Brown owns the CakeLove bakeries in the Washington, D.C., area and is a former Food Network star. As Tama Kieves put it in her book *This Time I Dance*, "If you're this successful doing work you don't love, what could you do with work you do love?"

The temporary dip in status is usually offset by such an increase in personal satisfaction that status becomes less relevant. Clare Dalton, a former tenured law professor, left academia in order to help heal people through acupuncture. She now has a thriving practice that she finds immensely rewarding. When Van Lanckton became a rabbi after practicing law for thirty years, he found a renewed sense of purpose, a supportive community, and an opportunity to serve in ways his legal career could never provide. Karina Gentinetta, a former law partner in New Orleans, says that she didn't "start really living" until she embarked on her current career as a designer and artist.

When I left my partnership, I struggled more with the loss of status than with the loss of income. I've found that people are more impressed by my excitement about the work I do than by my title because I light up when I talk about how bright and creative my students are and how much I enjoy teaching. Being truly engaged by your work is a more rare and impressive quality than being a lawyer in general.

A HIGHER PURPOSE

Many lawyers went into law to promote justice and advocate for the underrepresented. Some lawyers mindfully pursue those goals every day at legal services providers or nonprofits. Others find satisfaction in pro bono work. Many lawyers, however, leave the profession because they don't make the kind of impact they had hoped for. They went to law school intending to improve the world, and found themselves improving corporate profit margins instead.

At first glance, it can be hard to imagine finding a comparable sense of higher purpose in other fields. Practicing law is not the only way to effect change. It may not even be best way to create certain kinds of change.

Consider Jim Koch's experience. As chairman of the Boston Beer Company, whose Samuel Adams beers have won more awards than any other beer in history, Jim oversees a company of about 850 employees. While Jim was in law school, he was especially interested in environmental issues, and helped start the *Harvard Environmental Law Review*.

He considered practicing environmental law, but decided instead to join Boston Consulting Group. His first client was International Paper, which owned six million acres of timber and was at that time the largest private landowner in the United States. Jim soon realized that International Paper's forests were underused. He showed the company how to sustainably produce three times as much paper from the same land base.

As a result of Jim's recommendations, International Paper learned to increase the amount of pulpwood and timber it produced, without increasing deforestation. Other pulp and paper companies followed suit, taking the pressure off the forests Jim was so concerned about protecting. Implementing Jim's strategies effectively removed the threat that the forests would be clear-cut. "I could have spent my whole career as a lawyer working for the NRDC or the Sierra Club, and never had this kind of impact," he notes. Jim's experience shows that you can use the same analytical skills in business as in law, with potentially more effective and sustainable solutions.

There are many other ways to serve the public good outside of law practice. Not all of them require drastic pay cuts. Not all of them require drastic career changes, for that matter. If you move from an eighty-hour-a-week associate job to something with a less demanding schedule, for example, you may find more time to do something else that you find rewarding, whether that is being with your family, supporting a charity, or something that combines the two.

Many ex-lawyers find that the skills that made them successful in law translate well into development. Working to raise funds for causes or institutions you believe in can be as rewarding as being a legal advocate, if not more so. Meredith Benedict, for example, moved from a practice in health-care law to a successful career in development for Boston Medical Center before moving on to a start-up. She found that her ability to write compelling and persuasive arguments translated easily into writing successful grant applications. The skills she had honed as a lawyer served the hospital well, and Meredith moved up quickly to become the head of her department.

Another way to make an impact is to start a successful business and make charitable giving a part of it. Valerie Beck, who founded a series of chocolate walking tour companies, works with charity partners in every city she operates in. She missed having the opportunity to make a bigger impact in private law practice, and sees her charity work as one of the most gratifying aspects of owning a business.

With introspection and some amount of risk taking, there is no limit to what you can achieve outside of the legal profession.

3

CHALLENGES AND ALTERNATIVES FOR WOMEN LAWYERS

Women lawyers face unique challenges in the profession, along with at least one privilege. If success is defined as equity partnership and/or management roles, they don't succeed as often as men do. Some face a range of professional obstacles, including harassment and discrimination, which ironically are harder to overcome in a law firm than in other workplaces. At the same time, some women have something of an advantage over men when it comes to leaving their firms. Leaving a law job is easier to explain in conjunction with having a child than with having a change of heart. Many women who are unhappy in law practice may find a graceful exit in having children that isn't yet equally effective for men in most legal markets.

A FRUSTRATING STASIS AT THE TOP

Women don't make it to the top of private law practice in anywhere near the same proportion as they enter it. As the National Association of Women Lawyers (NAWL) reported in late 2012,

"Women lawyers leave law firms disproportionately more than men, at every stage."[1] While nearly half of law firm graduates are female, the percentage of female equity partners in large firms has hovered around 15 percent for most of the last twenty years. Because there are so few female equity partners, it's not surprising that there are even fewer women managing large firms. In fact, only 4 percent of large firms have a woman partner managing national operations. The dearth of women in high-level management means that it is especially hard to effect the firm-wide changes that might encourage more women to stay.

The issue of women's retention in law firms has been talked to death, with little real improvement. The rationales for trying to improve the number of women who stay are unarguable. Retention costs firms hundreds of thousands of dollars each year. It would be more cost-effective to try to keep promising associates than to replace them. Yet most law firms don't act rationally, at least on this issue.

The issue isn't one of quality, or that men make better lawyers. As the NAWL report pointed out, "The United States Supreme Court—certainly the most prestigious and vetted set of lawyers in the United States—has a far higher percentage of women members than equity partnerships in large U.S. law firms."

The problem is that women leave private practice in greater numbers than men. Some leave because the demands of law practice are inconsistent with the needs of their family. The billable hour demands of most law firms fundamentally limit lawyers' abilities to resolve the tension between work and home by working more efficiently. The business development pressures that increase as women grow more senior often require attending events in the evenings and weekends, adding to the time pressures for working mothers.

Some women leave because practicing law is uncomfortable, perhaps because they have few role models or champions within the firm who might increase their chances of promotion. Some leave because they have no viable way to address the discrimination or harassment they experience at work. Many women leave law for a combination of these reasons, although they don't talk about them in equal measure.

Women lawyers are also more likely to take time off from paid practice than men are. A recent survey of female Harvard Law School graduates found that more than a quarter of those currently working had left the paid workforce for between six months and three years at some point in their careers.[2] Most of these women took their time off for child rearing. A significant number stepped away because of illness, either their own or that of a loved one. Of the women who were no longer in the paid workforce, more than 35 percent had been out for ten years or more, usually for family care reasons.

THE GRACEFUL EXIT OF MOTHERHOOD

As we've seen, it can be hard for attorneys to leave their firms without a definite alternative, either in the form of a lateral move to a new firm or, less commonly, to change careers. Leaving law practice without either solid alternative can be perceived as failure, potentially erasing the goodwill that attorney has built up throughout her career.

Leaving the firm after a child arrives, however, is generally viewed as a fine decision for a woman lawyer. Some senior male partners may also see it as a more responsible choice than working full time. Often, these partners' wives work for pay part time or not at all. Such men may find it easier, on a subconscious level, to accept a woman who chooses to spend more time with her children than her colleagues.

I do not mean to suggest that anyone has a child primarily to facilitate leaving a firm. There is nothing wrong with leaving a career that doesn't accommodate your overall life goals; in fact, I strongly encourage it. For many people, including me, those goals change dramatically when a child enters the picture.

Having a child, whether it is her first or her fourth, makes it more socially acceptable for a woman to leave her firm than it is for a man. The financial and personal impact of those choices, however, affect women and men with equal force.

THE CHALLENGE OF REENTRY

When women take time off from practice for family reasons, it can be hard for them to regain professional ground if they return to practice. Traditional law practice effectively punishes women with divided loyalties. Having children is a twenty-four-hour responsibility for the primary caregiver, and not just when the kids are little. At the same time, many practice areas presuppose twenty-four-hour availability for supervising partners and/or clients. Something's gotta give. Illness, injury, doctor's appointments, parent–teacher conferences, early release days, and other family realities often conflict with the level of responsiveness most clients and firms expect from lawyers. As the population ages, and working women take on more responsibility for aging parents at the same time they are caring for children, the tension between caregiving and work demands are only getting worse.

The stress of trying to be all things to all people all the time can become unbearable. The double standard that honors men who take time to be with their children as wonderful fathers while diminishing women who do the same thing as uncommitted to their work still prevails in many quarters. Even women lawyers who manage successful careers with kids may never feel like they are doing anything well enough.

Taking time away from law practice can also change women's views of themselves and the legal profession, whether or not they leave for family reasons. Valerie Beck, for example, left law to become a Mary Kay representative before starting Chicago Chocolate Tours, the company she has now expanded to several other cities. After years of working in male-dominated law firms, being in a woman-centered environment had a powerful effect. "It allowed me to shed the person I wasn't," she explains. "I could finally be who I wanted to be."

Spending some time away from law can help clear your head, allowing you to think more purposefully and creatively about what you love. Christina Whelton had left criminal defense work behind when she helped a friend with her matchmaking business. That experience helped her see a potential career for herself in recruiting, and eventually to create her own biotech placement firm. Her experience shows that your first nonlaw job doesn't have to be your last, but it could be a useful stop on the way.

While a lot of women "off-ramp," there are few well-defined "on-ramps" back into practice. There is little accommodation in most law firms for women who want to return to law after time off. While many women can, and do, return to law practice, it is much more of an uphill battle than many women with children want to engage in. Career reentry programs for attorneys, such as Pace's New Directions Program, are too few in number. In this regard, the legal profession lags behind the accounting profession, at least in terms of institutionalized career flexibility. Accounting firms such as Ernst & Young offer maternity leaves of up to six months, flexible work schedules, and extended leaves of absence without loss of medical benefits.

Having children makes it more socially acceptable to leave a law career, but it is by no means the only issue that drives women out of law. Discrimination and harassment have pervasive and often silent effects on many women lawyers, and ultimately lead them out of the profession.

THE SUBTLETY OF DISCRIMINATION

Most women lawyers who encounter gender discrimination, sexual harassment, or both hesitate to complain about it, for a variety of reasons. There is often no way to report these issues without effectively tanking one's career, at least within that firm. Reporting also tends to mean reliving these painful experiences and challenging the hierarchy in ways that are still taboo. Few women have the desire to punish themselves for others' wrongdoing. Discrimination and harassment are therefore probably more pervasive than studies can detect. Even so, studies show that discrimination and harassment affect large numbers of women lawyers, beginning in law school and continuing throughout their careers.[3]

The decentralization of law firm management is a big part of the problem. The Human Resources Departments of law firms manage the beginning and end of associates' stays in the firm, but have little power to affect day-to-day working conditions. In most cases, associates are managed almost exclusively by partners who lead their cases. Junior partners, to a lesser extent, report to senior partners. An associate experiences moments of weakness, whether physical or emotional, at the mercy of the partner who supervises her.

Partners vary in their managerial skills, but few are trained in how to manage junior lawyers effectively. Management is rarely taught in school, and is not a particularly popular topic for continuing legal education. In many cases, the coup of working with an especially successful senior partner often means working for a manager with little regard for vulnerability.

A CASE STUDY

That managerial weakness may well include insensitivity to the potential effects of pregnancy. When Karen Leong (name changed), a senior litigation associate in a large Chicago firm, announced her pregnancy to her supervising partner, he was supportive. Karen was managing the trial team for one of the firm's largest clients.

When she developed complications five months into her pregnancy, the partners became a bit less supportive. Her stress levels were beginning to affect the fetus, and Karen's doctor warned her not to work so hard. Karen had always worked hard, however, and wasn't sure how to cut back. Plenty of other lawyers worked beyond what other people might consider normal limits. She was fairly close to consideration for partnership. The last thing she wanted was to show signs of what could be taken for weakness. She knew that the firm expected her to handle her responsibilities and bill her hours, regardless of the effects on her health.

As her pregnancy progressed, her doctor gave her written notes intended for her HR department, recommending that her hours be reduced. Karen knew that there was no practical way to do that. If she stayed home, the partners would expect her to work from there. The litigation department was staffed so leanly that no other senior associates were available to step in and help her. Even if there had been, she would not have been able to transfer either the knowledge she had gathered about the case or the trust she had engendered with the client over the years they had worked together.

In her seventh month, the building threat to her baby's health compelled Karen to ask for a week off. Doing so meant getting several layers of approval from senior management and grudging semi-consent from her supervising partner. While she was excused from billing, she was still expected to keep up with the case by e-mail and to accept phone calls from the team. The following month, the team was running a mock trial experiment in New York. At eight months pregnant, she could not fly there herself. Rather than conceding that she could not run the mock trial, she worked closely with the associates and consultants to make sure it would go smoothly. As the team boarded the plane for New York, however, the senior partner called her and demanded to know why she wasn't going with them.

Karen worked until the day she went into labor, and intended to take advantage of the firm's short-term, part-time option when her maternity leave ended. A month before her planned return, however, the litigation chair told her that the part-time option was off the table. It was a perk for high-performing attorneys, he explained, and some questions had arisen about Karen's commitment in the preceding six months. The firm would, however, be willing to take her back full time. She declined, and left the firm.

Had Karen been a secretary or even a paralegal, she would have been able to take time off as her doctor advised without significant ill effects on her career. If she felt that she were being punished for the effects of her pregnancy, she would have been able to go to the Human Resources office with her concerns. As a lawyer, however, decisions about her career advancement depended on input from the partners she would offend or inconvenience if she brought those concerns to light.

At the same time, Karen's story illustrates the complexity of many women's law firm experiences. Continuing to work against medical advice was her choice. So was leaving the firm, in the end. There is no clear fault on either side, but there is an inescapable tension between the humanity of lawyers and the rigorous client service orientation of many larger firms.

Women lawyers who work in relatively gender-balanced environments are less likely to encounter such problems. They are more likely to find working arrangements that let them integrate their identities as lawyers and mothers. As we've seen, however, women make it to the top of law firms so rarely that it can be hard to find gender-balanced management teams.

VIRTUAL LAW FIRMS AND FREELANCE NETWORKS

In some parts of the country, virtual law firms and freelance attorney networks are expanding options for women who want to practice law outside of brick-and-mortar firms. Many were started by women who wanted to find new ways to practice law after starting their families. Extrapolating from their own experience, they recognize the enormous talent in other women that traditional firms haven't been able to tap.

Freelance networks engage attorneys who work from home to support law firms, legal departments, and solo practitioners. Virtual law firms operate in a similar way, but their attorneys work directly for end clients who hire them in lieu of traditional larger firms. Both models charge clients a lower hourly rate than brick-and-mortar firms, but provide the same high-quality legal work.

These alternative models are especially attractive for women lawyers because they allow these lawyers to work from home, as their schedules allow, doing interesting work without face time or billable hour requirements. While most are not working full time, that is often as they want it.

Montage Legal Group

One prominent freelance attorney network is Montage Legal Group, based in southern California. Laurie Rowen and Erin Giglia get at least one résumé every day from an attorney who wants to join the network they founded in 2009.

Laurie and Erin met in the Orange County, California, office of Snell & Wilmer. In a bizarre twist of friendship, in late 2007 they discovered that they were pregnant at almost exactly the same time. After having their daughters two weeks apart, the two litigators decided to become contract attorneys, helping law firms with overflow work from home. In January of 2010, they added their first freelance attorney to their network. At first, their goal was to change the way people thought of contract attorneys by creating a network of experienced lawyers who had previously practiced at firms like Skadden Arps and Latham & Watkins. They soon realized that they were changing the way contract attorneys thought of themselves as well. By providing law firms with high-quality attorneys, whose photos and profiles appear on the Montage Legal website, Laurie and Erin created an attractive alternative for lawyers who wanted to do challenging work outside the confines of traditional firms. As successful business owners, their lives are only slightly less busy than they were when both were litigators. The key difference: they are growing their own business, providing top-shelf legal services, and improving the lives of lawyers across the country. They spend their days meeting with clients, working with their attorneys, speaking at events, and growing their business. They also find time to mentor law students on networking and career development. Importantly, they have more flexibility in the time they spend with their children, and they find genuine satisfaction in their work.

Custom Counsel

Custom Counsel is a freelance attorney network similar to Montage Legal, based in Portland, Maine. Like Montage, Custom Counsel matches law firms and in-house legal departments with freelance attorneys who work mostly from their homes. Custom Counsel also provides solo practitioners with vacation coverage and extra help when their workloads become unbearable. Both networks focus on finding attorneys who can hit the ground running with little or no training from the client.

When Nicole Bradick founded Custom Counsel, it wasn't easy to convince some of the more conservative New England law firms to rethink the way they did business. For example, while Portland is a relatively small legal market, Nicole considers it somewhat set in its ways. Many senior lawyers in the area had spent their whole working lives in a firm or in-house. They couldn't understand why talented lawyers would want to work anywhere else. Part of Nicole's early work was to demonstrate that lawyers who want a flexible schedule are just as intelligent, capable, and well trained as any other lawyers in the community.

When Custom Counsel launched in 2011, it had six attorneys. As of early 2013, it employed fifty lawyers spread across New

England, New York, Washington, D.C., and Chicago. All of its clients were repeat clients, a rare feat for any service business.

Corporate Legal Partners

Massachusetts-based Corporate Legal Partners offers a different model. Unlike Montage Legal and Custom Counsel, its attorneys work directly for corporate clients. Its founder, Patricia (Trish) Landgren, got the idea for her business while she was in-house at a large Boston-area company. When she went on maternity leave, she was asked to find her own replacement. One option was to hire a lawyer from one of the prestigious firms she consulted with, at several hundred dollars an hour. Another was to hire a contract lawyer whose qualifications seemed dubious. Wishing that there were some middle ground, she decided to create one.

The ideal solution, she thought, would allow companies to hire talented attorneys on a project-by-project basis, especially when the projects could be completed fairly quickly. It was easy to find a temporary accountant or a human resources staffer, but there was no way to hire a temporary attorney that you could feel good about. A virtual law firm could provide these services with much less overhead than traditional firms, resulting in dramatically lower legal fees for the company. At the same time, it could provide attorneys who didn't want to work in law firms with the opportunity to work on interesting projects for a short period of time.

Corporate Legal Counsel only hires attorneys who have the confidence and competence to work directly with clients and who understand those clients' business needs. Their attorneys are relatively seasoned, with the kind of high-profile firm experience that clients find attractive. They have to be self-motivated, efficient, and able to work well without secretarial support. Importantly, they need to be comfortable with part-time and occasional work. None of its lawyers, aside from Trish, works a full-time schedule.

THE NEXT WAVE

Montage Legal, Custom Counsel, and Corporate Legal Partners represent an important trend for lawyers, but can only employ a fraction of those who apply. The number of applicants is especially striking given that the firms don't currently offer benefits, as their attorneys are independent contractors rather than employees. That structure hasn't impeded their phenomenal growth. As they grow, so too will the numbers of lawyers who no longer have to meet billable minimums or commute to a traditional office.

To be clear, none of these groups hire only women, prefer to hire women, or engage in any kind of gender discrimination, to my knowledge. Most of the attorneys who join these networks are women because women represent the majority of people who want this kind of flexible work arrangement. If and when more men reject the framework of traditional law firms, the makeup of these virtual firms should become more gender balanced. The emergence of SwiftCounsel, a freelance attorney network based in San Francisco that engages more men than women, is a hopeful sign. Its founder, Andrew Amerson, started the network because he wanted more work flexibility when his first child was born. As more men feel free to make those choices, the profession may become more accommodating for everyone.

PART II

Repurposing Your Law Career

Many unhappy lawyers assume that they have few viable alternatives outside of law. As we'll see, that could not be further from the truth. There are former lawyers in almost every field, although they don't generally dwell on their J.D.s. There is a realistic way for you to change careers so that you genuinely like what you do, no matter how much time has passed since law school or how you have been spending that time.

Even better, you can change careers without starting from zero. You can put the skills you have honed as a lawyer to use in a new and more rewarding line of work.

Much depends on how you see the skills you bring to the table. Too often, lawyers don't appreciate the value of their skills outside of a legal context. Their identity is wrapped up in their job titles rather than the portfolio of skills they use in those jobs every day. They may see themselves as tax lawyers, patent prosecutors, or criminal defense attorneys instead of analysts, writers, consultants, and advocates.

This narrow view is a natural outgrowth of the professional gulch most lawyers work in. If you interact mostly with other lawyers, it can be hard to remember that other professionals use similar skills in different contexts. They're not writing briefs, managing litigation teams, looking up precedent on Westlaw, or arguing legal precedent. But they are writing articles, managing teams, researching industries, or speaking in front of colleagues, industry groups, and students. They use the same skills that lawyers do, in a nonlegal context.

Taking a broader, more creative view of what you enjoy and are good at is key to a rewarding career change.

There are three basic steps to repurposing your law career. The first step is assessing the skills you have most enjoyed using in law school, law practice, and other areas of your life. This requires introspection. Knowing the skills you like using is different from knowing what you're good at. You could be the world's best oral advocate, but if you don't actually enjoy standing up and talking in front of an audience, using that skill in another context may not be much of an improvement over practicing law.

The second step is matching your preferred skills to a different career. This requires research. This is where it helps to get input from friends, family, and perfect strangers who agree to meet you for a quick conversation. The next chapter, "Reframing Your Preferred Skills," demystifies the process and explains how lawyers can become especially effective at networking. Reading about the careers of other ex-lawyers, like the thirty profiled in part III, "The Role Models," may also inspire you to think of new directions.

The third step is repackaging your previous experience to showcase its value and versatility. This requires persuasion. Trial periods, internships, and other temporary measures can do much to fill any remaining gaps in experience that you might need in order to be a stellar candidate for your new dream job. We'll walk through each of these steps in the next few chapters.

4

REFRAMING YOUR
PREFERRED SKILLS

L et's face it: you could probably succeed at a number of other jobs. As a lawyer, how do you choose an alternative career? I struggled with this question for nearly two years after leaving my law firm. I hadn't done much productive thinking about what to do next before I left. I had spent long Saturday afternoons reading career books in cafés, but by Monday my plans would be no clearer.

The turning point came when I started to think in detail about what I had liked and disliked about my work throughout my career. With help from Richard Bolles's *What Color Is Your Parachute?*, I realized that the parts of my law career I had liked best could point me toward my next career. Skimming the book had done little for me, but completing Bolles's flower diagram, or what he refers to as "that one piece of paper," made all the difference.

Then my persuasive argument training kicked in. I realized that I could retool my résumé to show how some of my prior experience qualified me for another job in a completely different field. Once I had revisited my own skills and preferences, I could reframe them for potential employers.

Every lawyer has a unique confluence of talents, interests, and preferences that can point him in a new professional direction. Reflecting on the skills you have enjoyed using in the legal profession, as well as your personal interests, can help you think about how you may want to deploy those skills outside of law. Your experience using those strengths in law gives you a head start in finding and succeeding in your next career.

WHAT DO YOU LIKE BEING GOOD AT?

Lawyers use a finite number of skills and strengths in practice, regardless of their job title or place of work. These include research, writing, persuasion, advocacy, project management, and client counseling. Different lawyers gravitate toward and excel in one or more of these skills to a greater degree depending on which of their natural talents they most enjoy using. Most lawyers have more than one of the skills listed above, but they prefer using some more than others. People who make a successful transition out of law end up using the same skills that they enjoyed using as a lawyer, or on the side, in a nonlegal setting.

The first step in expanding your professional options beyond law practice is identifying the skills you enjoy using, regardless of how often you use them in your current job (if at all).

The word "enjoy" is critical here. There is a big difference between the skills you find rewarding and the skills that you don't particularly like to use. You could be the greatest legal researcher in the world, but if you never want to look anything up again, you should focus on a different strength. If you simply find other ways to use the skills other people praise you for but you don't enjoy, you run the risk of taking a new job that you are capable of doing but will come to dread eventually. That, in turn, will delay the "right" job search even longer.

Identifying the skills you enjoy using is critical to your career reinvention for two important reasons. First, it allows you to see yourself in a different light. Instead of seeing yourself as an anti-trust litigator, corporate associate, or district attorney, you can see yourself as an experienced researcher, analyst, writer, counselor, manager, and/or advocate.

The second reason is that it helps you show future employers your value in compelling detail. By focusing on the ways in which you have demonstrated success by using your preferred skills, you can divert attention from the fact that you may have only worked as a lawyer up to that point. It clarifies the value proposition of hiring you by underscoring how relevant your experience is to their needs.

A NEW LOOK AT CORE LEGAL SKILLS

If you can pinpoint what you've enjoyed doing, you can start preparing to do it in a different professional context. As a lawyer, you may have enjoyed using one or more of the following skills.

Writing

Many people go to law school specifically because they like writing, and law involves a lot of it. It can be disappointing to learn that writing legal briefs is entirely different from writing fiction or exposition. Some writers find that becoming good legal writers has a bad effect on their personal writing. Others find that the demands of law practice, with its billable hour requirements and its unpredictable schedule, quash their creative instinct or soak up the free time they might have dedicated to writing.

Writing is one of the most common second or third careers for former lawyers. Linda Fairstein, a best-selling crime fiction writer, is an ex-prosecutor. Elie Mystal and Kat Griffin became high-profile bloggers. Dan Kimmel left law to become a movie critic, and Bob Blumenthal became a Grammy-winning jazz critic after being a government lawyer for fifteen years. The "Writers" chapter in part 3 describes the varied careers of some of these ex-lawyers.

Analysis

Some people discover, on answering the LSAT's logic questions, that they have great analytical skills. Complex problem solving is the lawyer's stock in trade. Some lawyers can see the analytical framework of every decision more easily than other people. They have better insight than others into the parallels and distinctions between precedential cases and their client's case. They enjoy the process of comparison and inference, and they excel at creating strategy.

Lawyers who enjoy using their analytical skills have a wide range of nonlegal career options that capitalize on those skills. Analytical ex-lawyers have gone into consulting, policy work, and executive placement, among other fields where their problem-solving skills benefit their employers and clients.

Advocacy

Some people grow up hearing that they should become lawyers because they have an argument for everything. People who argue well may, in fact, make excellent legal advocates. They may have loved debate in college and moot court in law school. They may gravitate toward litigation because trial work looks glamorous, at least until trial preparation starts in earnest.

But advocates have a higher rate of burnout than many other lawyers. Legal services providers may find the suffering they deal with every day overwhelming at times. Like social workers, they work long hours for little pay on emotionally complex cases. Many move on to other fields after a few years.

Other advocates find that they get either too little or too much time in court. When they join the litigation practice of a private firm, they may find themselves fully occupied with legal research and document review, at least for the first few years. As they progress up the ladder, they may go to court occasionally and argue a few motions here and there, but the vast majority of their time is still spent in the office. Even at the partnership level, only a small percentage of private firm litigators appear in court more than once a month.

Other lawyers find their court schedule is too demanding. Christina Whelton, a former criminal defense lawyer who went on to start her own biotech placement firm, found her caseload and round-the-clock schedule unbearable over time.

Advocacy skills open many professional doors. Carol Rose practiced law in a firm before stepping up to become the executive director of the American Civil Liberties Union of Massachusetts. She now oversees the work of one of the oldest and most active ACLU chapters in the country.

Other ex-lawyers become advocates in entirely different fields. Jen Atkins went from law to nursing, spending several years at home in between careers. As a cardiology nurse at Boston Children's Hospital, she now advocates for the youngest patients at a critical time. One of her long-term goals is to become an advocate for improving health care on a national level.

Counseling

Some lawyers love the personal interaction involved in counseling their clients. The chance to use your knowledge to make a difference in someone else's life, as opposed to a corporation's bottom line, is one reason many lawyers take on pro bono work. Being of service is one of the most rewarding facets of a legal career.

If you like client counseling, there are a number of other professions you might enjoy more than law. Some lawyers become therapists, often after benefiting from therapy themselves. Will Meyerhofer, for example, became a successful therapist after practicing law at a Wall Street firm. The flexibility of setting your own schedule and working with clients in intentionally relaxing spaces can be attractive.

You may not need to get another degree to be a different kind of counselor. Many ex-lawyers become consultants. A seemingly small shift can make an enormous difference in job satisfaction.

Susannah Baruch shifted from working directly on the legislative process to public policy consulting. Others change focus entirely. Greg Stone, for example, is a media producer and consultant in the Boston area who spent several years in journalism before starting his own company.

Management

Many lawyers are fabulous case managers. Some love the managerial aspects of their work as much as or more than the content of the cases. These natural organizers might enjoy managing other kinds of projects or teams. They can apply the same skills to any number of professional structures or project management, regardless of whether legal issues are involved.

Many ex-lawyers who manage well make great entrepreneurs. They have the discipline to keep a lot of balls in the air at once, and their experience negotiating contracts gives them a competitive advantage. The "Entrepreneurs" profiles in part III may resonate with many of them. For the more risk-averse, there are all kinds of interesting positions within companies that require great management and organizational skills. It may be hard to find another position like the one Alan Rilla has, as caretaker of an island in Boston Harbor, but his job is another example of an interesting managerial role.

Research

The first thing most law students learn to do is find the law applicable to any given set of facts by researching precedent. Good students usually know how to do good research, although they may or may not enjoy it. Many lawyers like the challenge of finding the single case that anchors the argument in their client's favor. Public interest lawyers may use their research skills to learn about the regulatory environment as well as the individual players who can have the greatest impact on their issues.

If you enjoy research, but not law, you might want to investigate a career in foundation work, journalism, development, or academia. You can put your research skills to work in many other fields.

Thinking about the skills you enjoy using will only take you part of the way toward finding the right career. An important part of choosing your post-law path is intuitive. Meredith Benedict, one of the analysts profiled in part III, put it well:

> You also have to check in with your gut and reflect on whether a new direction feels right, even if it doesn't make sense to other people. In the end, your choice will or won't resonate with your passions, making it clear whether you made the right tradeoffs for yourself. You will recognize that you are most happy when doing the things you believe in most strongly—for some of us that is helping others, for others it is building a retirement nest egg or conducting research. It is deeply personal and individual for everyone. And it is subject to change as we continue to grow through our lives and careers.

You may already have a great sense of the skills you have enjoyed using, whether at work or in a volunteer role. If you're not sure how to do this assessment, the next chapter provides a more structured approach.

Once you define the skills you have and enjoy using, what motivates you, and the kinds of workplaces that best suit your personality, you have much of the information you need to choose a new career. The next step is persuading an employer that you have the best combination of skills and talent for the job you want.

5

WHERE TO START WHEN
YOU HAVE NO IDEA
WHERE TO START

I dentifying the skills you enjoy using is the first step in finding work you love. It's often surprisingly hard to do this, especially if you haven't liked your work in a long time. Many lawyers have trouble remembering what they enjoy, aside from distracting themselves. Depression, which affects lawyers disproportionately, can exacerbate this problem.

Friends and selected relatives can help with this process. When you ask people who are close to you what they think you're good at, you may be surprised at their responses. The key insight that led to Lisa Montanaro's career transition came during a late-night phone call with a close friend, who pointed out that Lisa had always been good at organizing. Lisa became a certified productivity consultant, motivational speaker, and life coach, and now has clients across the country. When Will Meyerhofer was an unhappy associate, his brother pointed out how good he was at helping friends and acquaintances deal with personal problems. Will is now a successful psychotherapist with a Manhattan practice.

GETTING IT IN WRITING

Directed writing can also help you sort out the skills you have enjoyed using. It can be surprisingly helpful to sit down with pen and paper, or keyboard and screen, and write a few paragraphs about past experiences you have found personally rewarding. Write out as many of these experiences as you can remember.

Before you stop reading, let me say that when I read books that ask me to write things down, I feel vaguely annoyed. I am often reading on a tablet somewhere, or while I'm waiting for an appointment, or in bed. In short, writing and reading are mutually inconvenient for me. I understand that you're not necessarily about to put this book down and go find pen and paper, but if you want to make real progress on your career transition I urge you to do this at some point soon. The act of writing, and of narrating your own experiences, can be a powerful spur to your memory.

What you should write, in more detail, is the brief story of each past experience in which something you did made you feel good about yourself. These can be experiences you had before or after law school, working for pay or as a volunteer. They can include your last vacation if, for example, you enjoyed researching and organizing it. Ignore accomplishments that mattered to someone else but not to you. As you think and write about each experience, pay attention to what you enjoyed and why. What steps did you take in each situation? What aspects of the experience were most rewarding? What outcomes changed as a result of what you did?

Each chunk of this writing can be done, or at least furthered, in the time it takes to leave the office for a latte. You can write a little bit in the fifteen minutes between the time you're ready to leave home in the morning and the time you really need to leave. It can be done in long stretches in cafés, if you have that kind of flexibility. But it needs to be done.

After you have written several stories about your own rewarding experiences, you'll be able to start looking for commonalities. You can analyze your own stories to figure out your favorite productive skills. Once you know what skills you enjoy using, you can extrapolate professional situations in which you might use those same skills more often, to greater effect, or in a context that you find more enjoyable overall. That, in turn, will help point you toward a career that will be more predictably and consistently rewarding.

Sometimes, people see little connection between what they have been doing professionally and what they truly love to do. That's not the end of the world. In fact, it may be the beginning of a particularly rewarding turnaround. Valerie Beck, for example, enjoyed taking her friends on a walking tour of the best chocolate shops she found in Belgium one weekend. She hated practicing law, but she loved chocolate. Valerie is now the founder of a multi-city chocolate walking tour company that hosts thousands of customers every year and partners with charities in every city where it operates. She didn't enjoy being a lawyer, but as she thought about what she did enjoy, she created the foundation for a business that capitalizes on her passions and strengths.

Don't despair if you come up with few work-related experiences you enjoyed over the course of your career, or if none of them relate to law. Just focus on what you did, why you enjoyed it, and what happened as a result.

IDENTIFYING WHAT YOU FIND REWARDING

When I did this exercise myself, I was surprised by how few of my stories related to how I had spent most of my waking hours since law school. I didn't take much pleasure in what I did well at work. What I did enjoy included the following:

- Creating and managing events for the alumnae network I had established as head of my local law school alumni association

- Making the closing argument in a trial where I represented pro bono a convicted felon who sued the City of San Francisco for violating his constitutional rights
- Writing my senior thesis in college and doing research in the library

Importantly, I got paid for none of those experiences, unless you count the pro bono closing argument. As I thought about why I found them rewarding, I realized that I enjoyed using different skills in each context, including:

- Organizing meetings and working with professional women to help other women
- Speaking to groups about issues I found compelling
- Researching and writing in a university setting

At first, I wasn't sure how to use these skills in a professional context. When I talked with other people, however, they gave me ideas. One of those networking conversations led to my next role, leading an angel investor group. That role required a fair amount of collaborating with professional women, leading meetings, and speaking to groups about the importance of investing in female entrepreneurs. I couldn't have invented a better job for myself, but I wouldn't have understood exactly why it was a good fit had I not gone through the kind of detailed self-analysis that I recommend to you.

SHOULD YOU SEE A CAREER COACH?

For some people, enlisting a career coach during a major transition can be enormously helpful. Career coaches can help improve your self-analysis and provide the discipline you may lack. They can also help you extract more data from personality and career aptitude tests. If you find yourself going in circles, or about to settle for a job you don't want, it may be worth at least talking with a career coach.

Career coaches can also help you identify potential new fields to explore once you have identified your strengths. While many lawyers are excellent researchers, there is no Westlaw of alternative careers. Lists of job titles can also be wildly misleading. A career coach can help jump-start the process of matching what you love to do with careers you might not think of on your own.

Finding a good career coach takes some sifting. Marcie Schorr Hirsch, a principal with Hirsch/Hills Associates, recommends looking for a coach with four different qualities:

1. A regular habit of gathering new information from disparate sources to maintain a broad awareness about what is going on in the world;
2. The ability to see patterns and find trends in large, complex data sets;
3. The creative ability to predict how your talents and values might translate into existing positions and jobs that could be created; and
4. A personal chemistry that engenders trust, since outcomes are usually better when the client enjoys the coach's style and company.

Getting a referral is the best way to find a genuinely and consistently successful coach. Referrals can come from many sources, including therapists, friends, colleagues, human resource professionals, and university career center staff. A professional certification, on the other hand, is no guarantee of quality.

Hirsch recommends looking at what coaches have published. "It gives you a good idea of how they think, how original and creative they are, and whether or not others hold them in high regard," she says. She warns against working with coaches who don't actively provide thought leadership on career and workplace issues, as they may not be up to date on today's work world.

For Mary-Alice Brady, an ex-lawyer who started an online community for entrepreneurs, using a career coach made a big difference in her transition. She found a coach by interviewing a few candidates, whom she had found through recommendations from friends, and choosing the one she liked best. Working with a coach taught her to be proactive in her job search, rather than simply reacting to the many opportunities presented to her.

One of the most useful parts of working with a coach, she found, was doing homework. Her coach asked her to answer this question in writing every day: "What did I enjoy today and what was a challenge to me?" Her written responses gave her fodder to discuss with her coach during the talks they scheduled every few weeks. Having someone else hold her accountable for her progress on a regular basis also helped her develop better career search habits.

Other kinds of external support can help as well. For me, the structure of Bentley's career transition support program turned everything around. Although I was sure I could do it all on my own at first, I ended up spinning my wheels for too long, losing months of salary before getting myself some help. One of the most useful parts of the program was a session in which several career search professionals helped us brainstorm about career alternatives we might not have thought of before. Having the framework of a program I had to attend regularly, with colleagues who were going through the same kind of transition, led me to think more consistently and creatively about my next steps. It also led, unexpectedly, to a personal connection with the people who would hire me to teach full time four years later.

Those personal connections can have a powerful influence on your professional future. They can help you get detailed information about what different roles and employers look like from the inside. They can also help you strengthen the alliances that will help you get the job you want, once you know what that is. In the next chapter, we'll talk about how even introverts can make these connections successfully.

6

HOW TO STOP WORRYING AND LOVE THE INFORMATIONAL INTERVIEW

The second step of your career reinvention is matching your preferred skills to other kinds of work. Once you know the skills you enjoy using, you can start finding more satisfying ways to use them professionally. Figuring out how to research other careers effectively can be daunting. How do you go beyond job titles and sector descriptions to figure out what people really do, so you can decide whether it is something you'd like to do as well? This is how: informational interviewing.

Informational interviews are short conversations between you and someone whose job, transition, or company you want to learn more about. By "conversations," I mean question and answer sessions in which you ask 90 percent of the questions and let the other person do 90 percent of the talking. This allows the person whose time you are taking up to talk about his work life, and most people like to talk about themselves. Importantly, these are not job interviews. They are part of your fact-finding mission. There is no better way to understand what a field really looks like than to learn from the people who work in it every day.

When I first started asking for informational interviews, I was shocked by how many people agreed to them. After years in large law firms, I found it stunning that people I barely knew were willing to talk with me about their work lives when they had nothing to gain. These people went out of their way to offer me advice and help me make other connections. Their kindness, and my lack of experience receiving it, reassured me that leaving law was the right decision.

One odd consequence of informational interviewing is that it can create two-way bonds. As it happens, people feel more kindly toward those they have done favors for than toward those who have done favors for them. This principle is known as the Ben Franklin effect, for the man who first articulated it. In other words, asking people to help you is a good way to ensure that they will be inclined to help you again later, unless you don't thank them properly.

Informational interviews also help you minimize career risk. The more you learn about another field, the more likely you are to make well-grounded choices about it. It's far better to learn that an interesting field is not right for you through a priori conversations than through your own unpleasant experience.

Luckily, I corrected my own course as a result of informational interviewing. One of the first fields I explored after law was development. I liked working with mission-driven organizations, and I enjoyed talking with high-net-worth people like the clients I used to counsel. My neighbor, one of the kindest people I know, is a leading development professional who generously arranged some introductions. At the same time, I started going to professional association meetings and making connections of my own.

As I learned more about development, I started to realize that I wasn't going to enjoy it as much as I had first thought. I wanted to like donor relations work, but I couldn't overcome my own resistance to asking for money. That realization was embarrassing at first, since so many people in development had offered to help me make the transition.

The people I had met while networking certainly wouldn't have been so hard on me. Most people understand that career transitions involve a lot of exploration. There is no shame in concluding that a particular field isn't right for you; in fact, that is a critical part of the process. You may explore several potential careers before finding the right fit.

THE LAWYER'S ADVANTAGE

Lawyers are especially good at informational interviews because they can put many of their legal skills to use in the process. One way to think of informational interviews is as a form of research. Your job in an informational interview is to come prepared with a few open-ended questions that will help you learn what the other person's job, company, school, or field is like.

Litigators can also put their deposition skills to work in this context. Having an informational interview is very much like the initial stages of a deposition, in which the lawyer tries to get the deponent to talk as much as possible about background matters in the hope of establishing a comfortable rapport. You will ask questions designed to elicit as much information as you can. As in depositions, you should listen closely to the answers and ask any follow-up questions that come to mind. Unlike depositions, of course, you're not trying to expose inconsistencies in their answers. Your contact usually arrives without defense counsel.

Even shy, introverted, or socially inept people can learn to do this well. I know this from personal experience. Because your primary goal is to ask questions, rather than talk about yourself, you can sail right through it once you have the process down. Your second informational interview will be much easier than your first, and the next will be a piece of cake (relatively speaking).

THE INITIAL APPROACH

Social networks are a good way to find contacts to interview. LinkedIn, in particular, exists largely to facilitate networking. You may also find promising contacts by asking friends, neighbors, and family members who they might know in a field that appeals to you. If you are interested in a particular institution, you may be able to do some cold calling, but you may get a lower response rate.

Once you know who you would like to interview, you can ask to meet. The best way to make contact with someone you have never met before is by asking a mutual acquaintance to introduce you. You can then follow up quickly with an initial e-mail request. In that e-mail, briefly introduce yourself and ask for a short meeting at your contact's convenience. Be brief; the whole e-mail should be only three to five sentences long.

If you have not already been introduced, the subject line is especially important. Ideally, this includes something personal that may catch the recipient's eye, like "Our Mutual Friend Sarah Shaw." It should not be something generic and tempting to delete, like "Request for Informational Interview."

Your e-mail should include a quick summary of how you know this person (e.g., your mutual friend speaks glowingly of him; he is a leader in his field; you read about him in your alumni magazine). It should also say briefly who you are (e.g., a former lawyer exploring the field of development, a fellow Wesleyan alumnus who wants to learn more about technical writing, a health-care specialist who would like to learn more about what it is like to run the regulatory program at Children's Hospital).

Then, of course, you should ask for a meeting. Assume that the person you're contacting is incredibly busy. Ask to take no more than fifteen minutes of his time, and suggest meeting for coffee at the place most convenient for him. Be as flexible as you can possibly be about when and where you can meet.

It may be helpful to include a question near the end of your e-mail. Informal research shows that people are more likely to answer e-mails that end with question marks, all other things being equal. Don't you agree? Your e-mail might look something like this:

Dear Mr. Adler,

Our mutual friend Jane Smith suggested that I contact you. I am making a transition into user experience design and would be grateful for the chance to learn more about your work at Mobiquity. Would you be willing to talk with me for fifteen to twenty minutes any time in the next few weeks? I would be happy to meet near your office, whenever it is convenient. What times might work for you?

Sincerely,
Ari Smith

Your acceptance rate for these e-mails, even perfectly crafted ones, will likely be less than 100 percent. In fact, even 50 percent is an excellent return rate, and 25 to 40 percent is more realistic. If you are actively looking for a new career, you might set a goal for yourself of sending out five such e-mails every week. That will probably give you a return rate of about two informational interviews a week.

Your contact may ask to see your résumé before the meeting so he can get a better sense of who you are. If you don't have a résumé you like yet, you can say that you're in the process of revising it and then send it along when you have a workable version.

Once you've agreed on a meeting time and place, make sure to provide your cell phone number so the person can reach you if he has to cancel at the last minute.

THE MEETING

Arrive at least a few minutes early to the meeting. Because people form first impressions quickly, and those powerful, immutable gut feelings can have important consequences, aim to create a great first impression.

The proper etiquette is for you, as the beneficiary, to buy your mentor-for-the-moment a cup of coffee or tea and whatever else she would like. If she offers to meet you for a meal instead of coffee, then by all means take advantage of the extra time that offers, but the meal should be on you, too.

The goal is to have a short, sweet conversation in which you learn something that adds to your mosaic of career information. If you make the meeting brief and pleasant, you'll be remembered well and get useful information. Conversely, if you overstay your time or put the other person on the spot, neither you nor he will walk away feeling good about the experience.

In your precious allotment of time, you should do very little of the talking. Most of the talking you do should consist of questions you have prepared in advance, though they should appear spontaneous. In other words, don't read your questions from written notes. Asking your questions becomes much easier the second time you do it, because the questions need not vary much from person to person. Have a pen and small notebook with you to jot down any notes.

A good question prompts your contact to give you helpful information. Some effective basics are:

"What do you like best about what you do?"
"What kinds of skills do you think are most important in order to be successful in this field?"
"Is there anything you wish you had known more about before you got into this field?"
"Are there other companies/institutions/programs that also do good work in this field, in your opinion?"

One of your final questions should help you expand your network. You might ask something like, "Is there anyone else you'd recommend that I talk with?"

Just asking those questions alone, listening carefully to the answers, and asking any follow-up questions may take fifteen minutes. When your time is up, thank the person profusely and leave. If you are urged to stay longer, go ahead, but be sure to respect your contact's time and don't overstay your welcome.

There are certain things you should never do in an informational interview. You should never ask for a job in this context, or even hint about a job indirectly. You should not ask your contact for general career advice. Questions you should *not* ask include:

"What do you think I should do?"
"What job would be right for me?"
"Do you have any suggestions about my résumé?"

If you have been asking most of the questions, the other person probably does not know much about you. If anyone you barely know has ever asked you questions like these, you know how uncomfortable it can be. Making your contact uncomfortable defeats one of your main purposes. It may also lead to ill-informed, if well-intentioned, advice.

THE FOLLOW-UP

You might be shocked by the number of people who expect a thank-you note within twenty-four hours of an interview, informational or otherwise. Maybe you wouldn't be shocked, because you're old-fashioned at heart like me. The increasing laxity that characterizes many social interactions is irrelevant in this context. You are making an impression on a particular individual who can help or hurt your career, and you want it to be as good as possible.

E-mail thank you notes are acceptable in most cases. That

said, nothing packs a punch like snail mail. Ideally, you will send a handwritten thank-you note and put it in the mail the day after your meeting. It's nice to have a stash of cards you love for this purpose. You can get great-looking ones in fifty-pack boxes at Target.

If your contact suggested someone else for you to talk with, you should certainly follow up on that suggestion. Talking with those secondary contacts can be valuable in itself. It also justifies a follow-up e-mail to your original contact, which should convey the following points:

- That you followed her suggestion and made the contact
- How helpful that additional contact was to you (exaggerate if necessary)
- How grateful, again, you are for her help

That kind of e-mail has a dual advantage in that it reaffirms your genuine interest in the field and reminds the contact of your general existence.

NETWORKING IN PERSON

I have never liked going to networking events when I wasn't hosting them. A room full of people I have nothing in common with? Cliques of people who are already in the middle of a conversation, and with whom I can't hope to make eye contact? It can feel uncomfortably like middle school. For introverts, especially those in the middle of a career transition, such events can be especially daunting. Nobody should have to talk about her professional trauma with strangers who like their own careers so much that they have come to a conference about them.

But let's say you're interested in learning more about a new field and you don't know anyone in that field yet. Its professional association puts on events every few months, which are open to the public. If there is a chance that going to one of those events will help you learn something you don't already know, you should at least consider going.

Going to these events is a valuable form of career research. The stakes are low. If you don't make any productive connections, you have only lost the admission fee and a few hours of your time. Your goal at these events is just to make the acquaintance of a few people who may be able to help you learn more about their field. It is not to sell yourself as one of them. It's just to establish the minimal level of comfort with someone else that allows you to exchange business cards.

Having business cards while you are exploring new careers is nice but not necessary. It is easier to ask for someone else's card when you can proffer your own, but it doesn't do much more to further your search. Fairly simple business cards with your home address, e-mail, and telephone number can be had inexpensively from a number of sources. It is worth the extra money to get the card company's logo removed from the back.

Before you go to networking events, it's helpful to develop a short answer to the inevitable question "What do you do?" It can be something as simple as "I'm a former lawyer transitioning into the field of [chemical engineering or whatever else they do]."

When you walk into a room full of strangers, practice your technique. Walk up to a person standing alone, introduce yourself, and ask something easy, like "What brings you to this talk?" or "Have you been to one of these events before?" Or walk up to a group of people and ask, "May I join you?"

As with informational interviews, learning something useful is a matter of knowing the right questions to ask. "What do you like best about your job?" can elicit a long and/or interesting response. So can "What do you like least about it?"

When people are nice enough to give you their card, by all means, write within the next twenty-four hours or so to tell them how nice it was to meet them and how much you appreciated their advice. If you can connect with them on LinkedIn right away as well, so much the better. The longer you take to reach out to your new contacts, the less likely they are to remember you, to believe that you're genuinely interested in their field, and to feel that it is worth their time to help you. You may think that these connections have forgotten you once they walk out the door, and you may be right. But you have nothing to lose by e-mailing them to show how polite and responsive you are. In fact, you have the following to gain:

- It demonstrates that you are genuinely interested.
- It gives the contact an opening to respond, making a more substantive connection possible.
- It allows the connection to find you easily a month or two later, when he hears about an entry-level position or a training program or something else that you would love to know about. Searching e-mail contacts or LinkedIn for your name is relatively easy. Business cards, in contrast, are less effective because they often get tossed at the door.

Conversely, failing to follow up can have a negative effect. I have often had the experience of meeting people at events and offering to talk with them about their career transition. When I don't hear from them afterward, to be honest, I feel disappointed rather than relieved. Many people genuinely want to help you. You just need to do a little legwork (or fingerwork) first.

7

ADVOCATING FOR YOUR
NEXT CAREER

Once you have identified your preferred skills and where you want to use them, you have to connect the dots for other people. The third step in the transition process is to show someone who can hire you how your skills, experience, and personal qualities will make his life easier.

Making the extra effort required to prove your worth in a field where your law degree will initially come across as irrelevant can be daunting. Being at a competitive disadvantage is a strange experience for a lot of lawyers, many of whom have excelled at everything they have put their hand to. You have to work harder than other candidates to show how your legal work experience prepares you for your new nonlegal career. You will have to focus more intently on the message that you are qualified. To do that, you need first to internalize that message, or at least fake it convincingly.

When you apply for jobs in organizations where you already have at least one personal connection, that connection may affect how carefully the hiring manager reviews your CV. When you're applying for nonlegal jobs where you don't have personal connections, it's especially important to make sure your CV is closely tailored to the job listing.

SEO FOR YOUR CV

Human resource professionals, who are regularly flooded with inappropriate job applications, usually look for certain key words and phrases in the résumés they review. They may scan the applications with software that tags only those that include the key words and phrases. The terms they look for are usually included in, or easily inferable from, the job listing itself. It is a good idea to use these words and phrases in both your cover letter and the CV itself. You can think of this as search engine optimization (SEO) for your CV.

The process is relatively straightforward. First, figure out what the employer is looking for. Start with the job description. Then tailor your CV to make sure that it contains many, and ideally all, of the job description's key words within the narrative of your entries. Because each job description is different, you may want to create a unique CV for each job you apply for. This business of tailoring your CV may be somewhat labor intensive, but the additional effort pays off in the increased likelihood of getting past decreasingly attentive human resources officers and the keyword search programs they employ.

At a minimum, you should create a unique CV for each field you are interested in. If you are considering both development and higher education administration, for example, you shouldn't use the same CV even though it describes experience that may be relevant to both fields. Instead, your "development CV" should make it painstakingly clear how each example of your work experience has prepared you to do prospect development, event planning, or whatever other aspect of development the job entails. Your "higher education CV" might underscore instead how the same experience prepared you for success in an administrative role at a university, using the terms that are unique to an academic setting.

DESCRIBING YOUR EXPERIENCE IN NONLEGAL TERMS

Lawyers moving into nonlegal fields have to be especially persuasive, as does anyone who is starting over. Fortunately, many lawyers are good at persuasion. In revising your CV for a nonlegal employer, your main task is to translate your skills and accomplishments into the language of the industry you are trying to move into.

Few nonlawyers understand what lawyers do. In fact, few litigators understand exactly what transactional lawyers do, and vice versa. It is unrealistic to expect anyone outside of law to understand exactly how you have spent your days in practice. This is especially true in a competitive job market. Busy people won't infer in your favor, especially when they have hundreds of CVs in front of them for each open slot. It is up to you to connect the dots.

To be clear, you should never lie about your experience. Instead, you should describe it in terms that reflect its versatility. You have flexibility in the way you describe even the most rarefied work experience. A former trial lawyer can, for example, change the emphasis of his work experience from litigation to management, or from representation to leadership.

Reframing your work experience requires you to break down exactly what you did in each job, whether it was paid, pro bono, or strictly volunteer, and describe your accomplishments in nonlegal terms.

Let's look at an example. Here's an entry from the CV of a mid-level associate describing his time at a large firm:

Managed case discovery for multinational companies. Coordinated patent, trade secret, trademark, and antitrust matters for leading biotech and software companies.

Advised key executives and in-house counsel on various legal issues. Selected as one of ten associates firm-wide to join appellate practice group. Second-chaired trial on civil rights issues and represented clients pro bono in political asylum and unlawful eviction cases.

While this entry might impress a law firm, it means little to other employers. Someone who has no prior experience with discovery can't be expected to understand what managing case discovery entails. Similarly, being selected to join an appellate practice group means little outside a law firm. While many lawyers understand that appellate practice involves a high degree of analytical skill, that is something employers outside the legal field are unlikely to appreciate.

This same experience, however, can be rewritten in business terms. Let's say this attorney wants to leave law and go into health-care administration. In that field, the attorney's project management and organizational skills will be relevant and useful. He may want to play up his analytical skills too. His experience working with biotech companies might be relevant to his new field, so he should bring that to the foreground. Conversely, he should ditch a lot of the specific legal terminology, such as "case discovery," "appellate practice" and "pro bono" (unless he is applying for a job where public service experience would help his candidacy). His experience may be more appealing to a health-care organization when rewritten along these lines:

Managed complex information-gathering process for multinational biotech companies. Effectively handled multiple time-sensitive projects, working with ten- to fifteen-person teams in locations across the United States. Consulted with key executives on various strategic issues. Recognized as one of the firm's top-performing associates based on analytical and creative problem-solving skills. Served as second lead on case involving protection of rights.

Alternatively, let's say a lawyer wants to convince a recruiting firm to hire her, even though she hasn't worked in recruiting before. Perhaps the recruiting firm is looking for someone with excellent interpersonal skills and the ability to find candidates and engage new customers.

With a little creativity, the lawyer can parlay her legal experience to satisfy these requirements. She can demonstrate interpersonal skills on the basis of work she has done with clients, colleagues, and people she has volunteered with. She might describe her experience counseling clients as conversations in which she drew out what the client wanted in ways that engendered trust. She can explain that she would apply these same skills to working with the recruiter's candidates and client employers as well.

You may not have extensive industry knowledge unless your legal work related to or served the industry in question. If you do have relevant experience in the industry, however, you should play that up. If you have been litigating cell phone technology patents and want to move into the mobile communications field, for example, you may be able to show more direct experience.

Of course, there are limits to what you can reframe. If you are a public defender or district attorney who has spent most of your career in the courtroom, it's not realistic to excise the word "trial" from your CV. But you can underscore your ability to oversee many complex projects simultaneously, as well as your persuasive and public speaking skills, since trial work demands all of those qualities.

FILLING EXPERIENCE GAPS WITH INTERNSHIPS

Many ex-lawyers use internships and trial periods to ease the transition away from law. Trial periods help employers reduce their risk in hiring you. They also help reduce your own risk by trying out a workplace you are not sure you will like.

The best time to suggest a trial period is after you have had some success in interviewing for a new job. One of the last barriers may be some hesitation about your track record, or lack thereof, in that field. At that point, you may be able to persuade an employer to hire you for a probationary period of anywhere from three weeks to six months. If the company isn't happy with your performance at the end of that time, it can let you go with no hard feelings on either side. The trial period reduces the employer's exposure to risk and underscores the point that you are flexible and easy to work with. It also gives you a chance to knock the employer's socks off.

A trial period can also help you assess whether this next career is right for you, even if you decide not to stay with that particular employer. Informational interviewing can only give you an approximate sense of how well a particular role will suit you. Sometimes the best way to determine whether a new career is right for you is to try it on for size.

You may also consider an intentionally temporary work experience. Depending on where you live, you may be able to find an externship program already in place. The externship is an integral part of New Directions for Attorneys, a career reentry program for lawyers offered by Pace University in New York City and its White Plains, New York, campus. Carroll Welch, a graduate of New Directions herself, works with employers to create externships. These externships allow New Directions participants to add recent, relevant work experience to their CVs.

MITIGATING FEAR OF FAILURE

As you persuade employers to take a chance on you, you may also have to persuade yourself to take the same chance. One concern many lawyers face is the fear that they may not be good at doing anything other than practicing law. Lawyers, on the whole, are a risk-averse group. In fact, one way of looking at law is as a risk-reduction profession. It often takes a few years to feel at least competent as a lawyer, a consequence of the disconnect between school and practice. When you finally feel competent, starting over again at the left edge of a learning curve can be daunting.

A critical element of career transition is choosing a new venture that builds on the skills you already have and that you enjoy using, as explained in chapter 4. By choosing a new career that builds on the skills you have already enjoyed using, you reduce the risk that you won't enjoy or be good at whatever you do next.

Some elements of your new career, however, may be totally unfamiliar, and you may have to learn on the job. Fortunately, you're smart and good at learning new things. If you can pass a Civil Procedure exam, you have the capacity to master unfamiliar concepts. Your challenge is to convince prospective employers that you have the basic skills necessary to do the job well, and that you can learn everything else as you go along. Even people who have more industry experience than you do have new things to learn in every role.

When I first took on my role as executive director of Golden Seeds, an angel investor network that funds high-growth, women-led companies, I knew nothing about angel investing. I had experience with many other elements of the job, however, like managing events and collaborating with a network of members. I had spent many years running member-based organizations as a volunteer, and I had a lot of experience working with successful women. I could demonstrate that I was a quick study, since every patent case I had litigated required me to learn some new technology.

Before my final interview with Golden Seeds, I learned the difference between angel investing and venture capital. After I was hired, I read the books my colleagues recommended. I learned a lot about angel investing by paying attention to the investment process and asking what I hoped were judicious questions. A year into my job, I felt more comfortable with my knowledge of the angel investing world than I had with my knowledge of litigation as a second-year associate.

STARING DOWN THE SKEPTICS

Many ex-lawyers find that other people can't understand or accept their decision to change careers. Even when you are comfortably settled in a new venture, people may ask rude questions like "Why would you ever stop being a lawyer?" or "What happened? Did you get fired?" If you go back to school for additional training, people may ask, "Are you going to be a professional student?" As annoying as these comments are, it can be worse when you can tell that people don't respect your decision but keep their thoughts to themselves.

Some former lawyers have flip responses ready. Greg Stone, an ex-lawyer who became a media consultant and producer, sometimes replies, "I wasn't making enough money as a lawyer" or "I thought there were too many lawyers in the world."

Others respond more directly. When Lisa Montanaro left law to become a professional organizer, some of her law school friends took offense. Lisa realized that their reactions had more to do with their own careers than with hers. "I would ask them if they were happy," she said. "If they were, I would tell them that I was happy for them, and that they should stay in law. I wasn't, so I was leaving." Developing the courage to respond that way took time, but made her feel much better.

The good news is that this problem diminishes over time. "People don't take you seriously until you're successful," says Greg Stone. "People may not understand what I've done, but when they see that I've made a go of it they respect me more. You just need enough confidence to deal with it on your way up. It takes time to be successful." Still, it may never go away entirely. Nathaniel Stearns left law twenty years ago, and his mother still asks every now and then when he might go back to it.

In the next section of this book, you'll read about the experiences of lawyers who went off the beaten path. The universe of former lawyers expands daily. In reading about the wide range of other options available to you, I hope you will find a role model whose interests and goals resonate with your own.

PART III

The Role Models: Eight Basic Paths to Career Happiness for Former Lawyers

Lawyers can succeed in a variety of other professions that they may enjoy more than law. The thirty former lawyers profiled in this section made rewarding career transitions in very different ways. Some left law almost immediately, while others stayed in the legal world for thirty-five years or more. A range of factors influenced their career decisions, including personal dissatisfaction, family priorities, health problems (whether their own or a loved one's), growing interest in a different field, and the driving need to make their lives more meaningful.

My definition of a successful career transition has little to do with fame or wealth. Some of the former lawyers profiled here are internationally famous, and many others aren't well known outside their community. Their transitions are successful because they enjoy their new careers more than they enjoyed practicing, teaching, or studying law. They are doing what they want to do instead of what they should do according to someone else's metrics. In nearly every case, they use the skills and strengths they had drawn on in the legal profession in new and more rewarding ways.

For most, it took some time to establish a new career. Many tried other kinds of work before settling in to what they do now, illustrating the point that your next move need not be your last move. Some went back to school for another degree or certification, but most did not. Some simply needed time away from law practice before they could think clearly about what they really wanted to do. Few of them regret having become lawyers, although many wish they had left sooner. In every case, to varying degrees, they leverage their legal skills in their new careers. Most see the practice of law as one step along the path to where they are now.

Although every career transition is unique, I have grouped these lawyers' stories into eight categories according to the kinds of skills they most enjoyed using. You will probably find that you resonate more with some of these groups than others. The groups include:

The Writers, who write in a variety of formats and genres

The Entrepreneurs, whose innovations led them to start companies of their own

The Artisans, who create new work with their hands

The Analysts, whose ability to manage and interpret information drives their success

The Professors, who use their research and oral advocacy skills to train the next generation

The Consultants, who combine their counseling skills with substantive knowledge

The Advocates, who work to further the interests of an underserved group

The Healers, who have found more satisfying ways to help people than by representing them

These categories aren't meant to limit your possibilities in any way. I've included a bonus profile of someone whose career shift defies categorization, because his story is too much fun to leave out.

All of these former lawyers can serve as role models for other lawyers who want to make a change, but may not yet know how.

8

THE WRITERS

Many people who go into law would have loved to become writers, if only there were a steady writing job market that offered similarly great pay, benefits, and social status. For these lawyers, writing would be the best part of their job if they were not writing briefs, contracts, and research memos. Some of them also enjoy the research aspect of law and the scholarly process of crafting a well-informed motion.

Some of these lawyers find their next career in writing. There are former lawyers in every genre. Adam Liptak, the Supreme Court correspondent for the *New York Times,* worked for ten years as a lawyer before becoming a full-time journalist. Stephanie Rowe, one of Amazon's top-selling indie romance novelists, is a former lawyer who spent years working for Nike's research and development group before she started writing full time. For Nathaniel Stearns, the right career was a combination of being home with his children and writing and advising about eighteenth- and nineteenth-century American art.

Some lawyers become bloggers, writing about subjects that may be related or unrelated to the legal profession. Elie Mystal left his prestigious Manhattan firm to become first a blogger and then the editor of *Above the Law,* perhaps the most popular blog for lawyers. Kat Griffin is the ex-lawyer behind *Corporette*, a blog that offers "fashion, lifestyle, and career advice for overachieving chicks."

All of the lawyers-turned-writers profiled here spent months, and in some cases years, writing on the side before they were able to write for a living. Adam Liptak had contributed a number of pieces to the *New York Times's* weekend sections before he became the paper's national legal correspondent. If he hadn't established his ability to write well, he might not have gotten the offer to write consistently. Adam's first job at the *Times,* however, was as a copy boy after college.

Adam Liptak, *New York Times* Correspondent

Adam Liptak practiced law for fourteen years before becoming a journalist full time. He didn't particularly like working with many of the clients he represented at Cahill Gordon & Reindel, the firm he joined after law school. He never liked discovery or depositions. He enjoyed analyzing the underlying materials of a case and the solitary nature of writing about the result. Those preferences translate perfectly to his current role as the Supreme Court correspondent for the *New York Times*.

Adam sees his years practicing law as a long detour from journalism, his first love. He wrote for the *Yale Daily News* and set his sights on becoming a journalist. He applied to law school as a fallback. By the time he got his acceptance letter from Yale Law School he had already landed a job as a copy boy at the *New York Times*. He deferred his acceptance, thinking that the *Times* job could be a great start for his journalism career.

He soon realized that most of his job involved clerical work and fetching coffee rather than actual reporting. His only significant reporting opportunity came from helping M.A. Farber, a reporter he admired, cover a libel trial. Reporters could not file stories from the courthouse, so Farber would return to the newsroom in the late afternoon. When Judge Pierre N. Leval kept the trial in session until six p.m. or later, Adam got his chance to fill in. He would go to court as Farber was leaving, and call in to report what happened at the end of the day.

After some months of this, Adam became frustrated. It was clear that the *Times* wasn't going to hire him as a reporter. The more traditional route then would have been to go to a regional newspaper, get more experience, and work his way up, but that didn't appeal. "I had been to Yale. I was already at the *Times*. I didn't want to leave town and go to work for a less prestigious outfit," he says. He reconsidered law school, and decided to go become a libel lawyer. "It seemed like a way to be near journalism even if I couldn't be a journalist myself."

Adam liked his Yale Law School classes and classmates. He enjoyed legal writing and research. Big law firms came to campus, offering tremendous salaries and nice offices. "Why not take the easy path?" he wondered.

Adam spent his second summer at Cahill Gordon & Reindel working for the legendary libel lawyer Floyd Abrams on First Amendment cases that he loved. When he joined Cahill after graduation, however, he was assigned to less engaging cases. In his fourth year, he had a decision to make.

A rare job had opened up in the *Times*'s legal department. While this seemed like an incredible opportunity, he was doing well at Cahill and thought he had a good shot at making partner. For most of his colleagues, partnership was the ultimate goal, and Adam had started to internalize those values. On the other hand, he had no particular affection for his clients. Given the choice between the *Times* and the investment banks he had been defending, Adam thought, "I'd rather represent the *Times*."

Working in the *Times*'s legal department was less exciting than he had expected. At first, he missed the intense problem solving that had been part of his previous firm's culture. He was no longer surrounded by people at the top of their intellectual game, as he had been at Cahill. On an in-house team, he had to be more cautious about his time and the department's resources. On the other hand, he got to work with journalists every day. His job at the *Times* offered him reasonable amounts of money and status, and he had more time to see his family than he would have had as a Cahill partner.

After several years in the legal department, Adam's job started to feel repetitive. Much of his work involved checking stories to spot potential libel problems, which were rare because the *Times* reporters were so good. "I felt like the Maytag repairman," he says. "It was a little boring because there wasn't much to fix." He often found time to write articles and book reviews on the side. Many were published, including pieces he wrote for the *New York Times Book Review* and what was then called the Week in Review section.

The monotony of his work started to wear on him, but he wasn't sure what to do next. At forty-two, he didn't want to go to a firm. Corporate legal work no longer appealed to him. He talked with the *New Yorker* about joining its in-house legal department, but concluded that if he was going to do the same kind of work he might as well stay at the *Times*.

As Adam was trying to plan his next move, he got a stunning offer. Howell Raines, then the executive editor, asked him whether he would like to be the *Times's* national legal correspondent. According to Adam, "He offered me my dream job." He still isn't sure why Raines took a chance on him., though he suspects that the offer wouldn't have come if it hadn't been for Adam's steady stream of writing. He quotes a judge who once told him, "If you want to play, you hang around the hoop and you hope someone gives you the ball."

The joy of getting his dream job was followed by what he describes as "six months of pure terror" as he learned how to do it. Even so, it was the right move. "I had a distinct feeling that it was good to do more than a few things in life, even if this next thing didn't turn out to be better," he says.

In his first year, Adam went from being at the top of his game as a lawyer to being on the low end of the learning curve as a reporter. "I had more than my fair share of corrections that year," he said. Among other things, he had to get used to writing on deadline. He recalls one editor telling him, "We know you can write well. Now we'll find out if you can write fast."

His skills in legal research and writing served him well, and he had good instincts about what makes a story compelling. He did so well that when Linda Greenhouse, then the *Times*'s Supreme Court correspondent, announced her retirement in 2008, Adam was offered her job.

The promotion was something he had expected and feared. This was a spectacular assignment for a journalist who likes law, but it would mean moving to Washington, D.C. Adam had been in New York for a long time and didn't particularly want to move. He was also hesitant about going from a wide-ranging beat to one with a relatively narrow focus. In the end, he thought, "How can you say no to a job like that?"

He found a lot to like about becoming the *Times*'s Supreme Court correspondent in 2008. The quality of the argument is unparalleled, he says, and the justices are fun to see in action. He also enjoys being part of a relatively small community, or "groupies," as he describes them, sharing an obsession with all things associated with the court. Because there are so few exclusive scoops, he notes, it's not as competitive as most assignments. On the flip side, it's harder to come up with distinctive stories.

Adam advises lawyers who might like to write not to get accustomed to law firm salaries. He also encourages them to get as much writing experience as they can, even while they have a day job. "If you want to write, you have to write, and write as much as you can," he says. "Ideally, you should write with something fresh to say, not just a piece for your firm's newsletter." Adam compares writing to using a muscle: the more you do it, the stronger it gets.

Adam's experience illustrates the importance of building up a portfolio of published work before you look for a full-time writing job. The accessibility of blogs makes it easier to do this than ever before. Mike Sacks, for example, wrote about the Supreme Court on his own blog, *First One at One First,* while he was holding down a less than thrilling day job. The premise of his blog was that he was the first to review the Supreme Court's docket when it was posted each morning. On the strength of his blog, *The Huffington Post* eventually hired him to be its Supreme Court correspondent.

Other people leave law to run a blog of their own. Kat Griffin, whose blog, *Corporette,* is one of my favorites, is among them. I had been reading *Corporette* for months before I realized that Kat is a former lawyer too. Like many other writers, Kat held down a full-time job while writing her blog for years before she felt comfortable leaving her law job. *Corporette* was number two on *Forbes's* list of the Top 10 Lifestyle Websites for Women, and has been mentioned in the *New York Times,* the *Financial Times,* the *ABA Journal,* CNN, Oprah.com, *Lucky* magazine, and more. With the success of *Corporette,* Kat's writing allows her more flexibility than any legal job she can imagine. It's also much more fun.

Kat Griffin, Founder and Editor-in-Chief, Corporette.com

Kat Griffin is the force behind *Corporette,* a blog offering fashion and career advice to lawyers, investment bankers, and other high-achieving women. Writing *Corporette* allows Kat to combine her long-standing love of writing, her big-firm litigation experience, and her eye for style to mentor other young professionals.

While Kat didn't grow up wanting to be a lawyer, there were subtle hints at home. Her father was a patent lawyer. When she was nine, Kat put on a puppet show for her class explaining the different kinds of intellectual property. Her parents encouraged her to take the LSAT before she had even started college, but she was drawn to journalism instead.

The idea of law school only appealed to Kat after college as she considered writing about the Digital Millennium Copyright Act. She was pitching a story about it as a freelancer when she realized that she could build a law practice around it instead. Digital law was a growing field. By establishing a niche in an area she loved, she thought, she could avoid the drudgery she saw in so many other law careers.

At Georgetown University Law Center, Kat's focus changed from copyright law to the First Amendment. After graduation, she went to work with Floyd Abrams at Cahill Gordon & Reindel. There, she was assigned to interesting cases, including a Supreme Court petition involving the investigation of Valerie Plame.

As engaging as those cases were, Kat realized that litigation wasn't right for her. She was doing well, but it was a constant struggle. "It never came easy to me," she says. She considered going in-house to a media company. As she started to look for those jobs, she heard about a different opportunity. There was an opening at the Media Law Resource Center (MLRC), organizing conferences and writing about cutting-edge media-related issues. Having spent her 1L summer working for the MLRC, she had experience with its mission and connections to its leadership. She left Cahill for MLRC in her sixth year.

At the same time, Kat started a fashion blog for lawyers. She felt there was a near-total lack of guidance for high-achieving women on what to wear to work. There was no reliable source of advice, for example, about the best T-shirts to wear under suits or which shoes both looked good and let you be on your feet in front of a jury for several hours. Most fashion advice was irrelevant to her working life.

Kat's new blog was intentionally fun to read. About six months before she started blogging, Kat took a class on humor writing. Taking that class reintroduced her to a side of herself that was underused in her law career. "As we get older, we stop doing things for pleasure or joy, but because we think they're going to look good on our transcript or résumé," she says. "Finding time to reconnect with your core sense of self can help open things up on an unconscious level."

At first, Kat did all of her writing at five a.m. because that was the only time she had free. She had to learn the basics of putting each post together. "At first, it would take me an hour to post a photo," she says. Although she had told Cahill about the blog early on, her readers didn't know who she was. She wrote anonymously in order to keep as many professional doors open as she could. She didn't introduce herself to her readers until March 2010, almost two years after *Corporette* launched.

Kat grew her initial audience by asking thirty people she knew to check out the blog, suggesting that she had heard about it herself. As her audience grew, Kat expanded her subject matter to include career advice directed at summer and junior associates. She had seen some younger lawyers tank their own careers by saying or doing the wrong thing because they didn't know better. She saw a need for advice presented in the light tone that younger professionals might internalize. One of her most popular posts explained, for example, the proper etiquette for business meals. "I thought of it as writing to myself at twenty-five about all these things I wish I had known then," she says.

The blog didn't make money right away: it was largely a labor of love. It wasn't until the blog's fourth year that Kat felt comfortable giving up her day job at MLRC to write full time. As she attracted more readers and advertisers, the blog started to make money. Now, she says, "It is far more lucrative than anything else I could be doing for thirty hours a week."

As her blog grew, Kat learned about the potential income from affiliate marketing. If Kat recommends a sweater from a particular store, for example, and posts a link to the store's site, she can get a cut of any sale that results from clicking on that link. "I had no idea that that existed when I started the blog. I just lucked into it," she says.

Kat was surprised at how rewarding her blog became. She had written cover stories for *Family Circle* magazine as a freelancer before law school, but this was better. "It was much more satisfying to write a post and know that three hundred people had read it than to have a story on the cover of a national magazine," she says. It got better when her readers started e-mailing her for advice. Answering their questions about clothing and etiquette came more easily to Kat than practicing law ever had.

As Kat describes it, she works at an odd intersection of popularity and anonymity. To her 140,000 loyal readers, she is well known, open to both praise and devastating criticism. Highly articulate professional women, her target audience, can be blisteringly harsh in their disapproval, and the anonymity of the Internet only makes it worse. "Nothing quite prepares you for the thick skin you need to work on the Internet in a creative capacity," she says. "Law didn't prepare me for it."

At the same time, people who don't read her blog tend to undermine her work. "When you tell people you're a blogger, it doesn't give you much credibility," she says, "especially compared with telling people you're a lawyer with a Wall Street firm." While some people know that bloggers can make money, they also know that most bloggers don't, and most can't tell whether she is one of the lucky few.

In addition to building a successful business, Kat is particularly proud of giving good advice. She values the e-mails she gets from young lawyers who tell her how *Corporette* helped them get a promotion, or helped them become more financially savvy. "Those e-mails make feel like I'm doing some good in my little corner of the Internet," she says.

One striking part of Kat's transition was the effect of taking a comedy writing class. The class helped to free up the naturally funny writing voice that law and policy work may have muted. It also helped build her confidence as a writer, which almost certainly made her blog more successful.

Taking a class, like Kat did, or joining a salon can be an excellent way to get back to writing, especially if you haven't been able to carve out much time to write. When I practiced law in San Francisco, I joined the Red Room writing salon run by Ivory Madison, herself a former lawyer. Every week, several of us would sit around a large table in a mansion off of Alamo Square and just write. It was silent. There were tea and snacks. It was the best time of my week. It allowed me to reconnect with myself as a writer and to find a community of other writers, even though I didn't try to publish anything until years later. I did, however, take part in National Novel Writing Month that November, which I highly recommend. My novel was awful, but the experience was fun.

While Kat started blogging before she left MLRC, other successful bloggers start after they leave law entirely. For Elie Mystal, it took a clean break from his top-tier Manhattan law firm and the experience of starting over again completely. Many months of writing, mostly as an intern, helped him develop the writing voice that would ultimately make him successful. His writing experience helped him win the popular vote that allowed him to blog full time for *Above the Law,* where he is now its editor.

Elie Mystal, Editor, Abovethelaw.com

Elie Mystal is the editor of *Above the Law,* one of the most popular blogs on the legal profession. He was the first winner of "ATL Idol," the competition in which readers voted to narrow a field of potential writers. Before he went to ATL, he was a Harvard-educated litigator at Debevoise & Plimpton.

Elie says he went to law school "because I was good at school and I didn't want to start working right away." After majoring in government, he worked as an assistant press secretary for Hillary Clinton. He liked the public discourse of politics, and thought that he might run for office himself someday. "Law school was supposed to be a good idea if you liked politics," he says. His parents pointed out that there would always be opportunities to work for another candidate, but he should get law school out of the way as soon as possible.

"I got a very high score on the LSAT, and I didn't look up again until I was leaving my law firm," he says. At Harvard Law School, he was stunned to learn how much large law firms paid. Elie was not raised by wealthy parents. "The salary they were throwing around, even for first-year associates, was more than my parents ever made," he says. He landed an offer from Debevoise & Plimpton. He recalls one particularly impressive meeting with a partner, who leaned in and told him, "The doors to the world of Debevoise & Plimpton swing open only once."

The money was almost impossible to resist. Mindful of how many sacrifices his family had made for his education, Elie accepted the offer. "I felt like I owed it to my family, and to myself, to earn that much money," he says. He told himself it would just be for a few years, and then he would get back to politics.

He joined the litigation practice, specializing in regulatory defense. In almost every case, his clients ended up firing someone internally. He found he had a knack for sifting through documents and figuring out who the victim should be. While he enjoyed the partners' praise, he also felt a bit like the grim reaper. "It was not a particularly positive experience," he says.

Elie liked nothing about being a lawyer. He thought *stare decisis* made no sense. "Why should I care about what an old white man thought fifty years ago?" he says. He never saw the point of string cites. He resented the artificial deadlines that resulted from case mismanagement. It was also hard to form real friendships, since so many people checked their personalities at the door in the morning. What he liked least was the hours. "There is nothing I want to do for fourteen hours straight every day, no matter what you pay me," he says.

His decision to leave was sudden and involved Las Vegas. Elie had been working particularly long hours on one case. When he came into the office one weekday, a partner came to his office and told him that the case had been settled the night before. The partner encouraged him to go home and take a shower, and maybe go to the beach for the day. Instead, Elie got in a cab, went to La Guardia, and took the next flight to Las Vegas. In Vegas, Elie realized that if he continued to work at the firm, he would probably do something like buy a house that would bind him to his salary indefinitely. Now, he thought, was the time to get out. When he told his wife, who is from Zimbabwe, that he wanted to quit, she agreed. They had gotten used to living on one salary while they were waiting for her work visa to come through. She was now doing well at J.P. Morgan, and they could go back to living on one salary.

When he told the firm that he was leaving, they discouraged him. To his amazement, they gave him a six-month paid sabbatical so that he could think about his next steps. "So I sat on my couch and played video games," he says. He thought about going back to politics, but realized that he no longer wanted to work around the clock for someone else, even for someone or something he believed in.

When the six months was up, one thing was clear: he wasn't going back to a firm. The problem wasn't Debevoise in particular, he realized, or even regulatory defense. He just didn't like practicing law. "Deciding I did not want to go back to law was easily the best decision I made in my legal career," he says.

During his sabbatical, Elie had started writing. At first, he wrote a blog. "It was terrible," he says. He applied for writing jobs at the *New York Times* and the *Washington Post*, but nothing panned out. For someone who had always succeeded at the most prestigious institutions, rejection was a new and unsettling experience.

"I have to credit my family for sitting me down and telling me to be more realistic," he says. He set his sights lower, and sent his résumé to every publishing company in New York. His cover letter explained that he was highly educable, and that he was willing to work for free.

His only response was from someone who promised to teach Elie everything he would have learned in journalism school. Elie took the offer. "After all," Elie says, "I had gotten one graduate degree on a lark and I didn't want to do that again."

Six months later, Elie got a job writing a legal column for a politically oriented publication. It felt good to have his own byline, the first outward sign of his success as a writer. Although the newspaper had layoffs, he understood that his column was safe because it would have been hard to find another writer with the same legal and political experience.

One day, a friend told him that *Above the Law* was holding a contest to find a regular contributor. Every week, readers would eliminate one of the contestants, and the one who remained at the end would be given a regular spot. Elie had been reading ATL since he left Debevoise. He applied to the contest and won.

Elie credits his writing internships, rather than his legal background, to his success. "The other contestants were also lawyers, but they hadn't had as much experience writing a column," he says. ATL suits Elie because he likes writing about what lawyers think, rather than about the substance of law itself.

Elie's advice to unhappy lawyers in private practice is not to stick it out. "If you are thinking of leaving your firm, don't stay for a few years. Do it now," he says. The golden handcuffs are real, he says, and people tend to underestimate how much harder it gets to walk away as life unfolds. Changing careers is hard enough, according to Elie, and you never know what may happen to make it even harder. "You could have a baby," says the new father, "or you could have an accident."

Blogging, of course, is not the only option for lawyers who want to write. Many lawyers write novels, and some become bestselling authors. One example is Linda Fairstein, the former head of the sex crimes unit for the Manhattan District Attorney's office. Fairstein's series of crime novels featuring prosecutor Alexandra Cooper became international best sellers.

Another example is Stephanie Rowe, whose contemporary and paranormal romance novels have won her industry-wide accolades and top-selling status on Amazon. Writing is actually Stephanie's third career. Her first was corporate law.

Stephanie Rowe, Fantasy and Romance Novelist

Stephanie Rowe's story illustrates the power of persistence. Now a successful writer with an enormous fan base, Stephanie wrote eighteen books before she sold her first one.

When Stephanie decided to go to law school, it wasn't with the goal of practicing any specific type of law. She had dated a law student and found his studies interesting. She enjoyed law school because it was a good fit for the way her mind worked. The practice of law itself wasn't nearly as much fun.

She joined the corporate practice of a large Boston law firm, where she stuck it out for a year and a half. Thinking the problem might be the firm itself, she transferred to another large firm, but left after six months. "The decision to leave was easy," she told me, "because I was miserable. The hard part was figuring out what to do next." Billing so many hours, she had had little time to think about other options. She decided to take some time off.

Stephanie had always been athletic, and after leaving her firm, she played a lot of tennis and tested tennis shoes for

Nike. Stephanie enjoyed her interactions with the company. When her family went on vacation near the Nike headquarters in Oregon, she thought it would be interesting to see behind the scenes. She used her connections with the research and development department to arrange for a tour.

When she got there, she found that her contact had also arranged for a meeting with the head of Nike's product-testing department. Stephanie was surprised, but treated it as an informational interview. At the end of the hour-long meeting, he told Stephanie he had a job opening, and suggested that she apply. Crazy, right? Stephanie applied, got the job, and moved with her family from Boston to Oregon three weeks later.

Stephanie later learned why she had been singled out to meet the department head. As a Nike product tester, her unusually detailed reviews set her apart from other testers. As she puts it, "I was one of their favorites because I was an over-achiever."

Stephanie worked for Nike's product-testing department for eight years, eventually becoming the head of the depart-ment. She appreciated the promotions, but did not want more of them. "I didn't see myself following any of the more senior career paths at Nike," she says. "It's an internationally based company and I would have had to travel all the time. That wasn't consistent with my desire to have kids."

She wasn't sure what she wanted to do next. High on her priority list were intellectual challenge and complete control of her schedule. She came up with a list of potential career ideas, including training seeing-eye dogs, becoming a tennis instruc-tor, and writing novels. After reading an article in her college alumni magazine about another alumnus who had sold the movie rights to her book, Stephanie decided that she could write a book too.

Because she didn't have a personal computer at first, she started going in to work early and staying late in order to write there. She wrote her first book that way. Three years later, she was still writing morning and night, and working full time at Nike. She wrote eighteen books but couldn't sell any of them. She received almost two hundred rejection letters before her first sale.

Her luck changed when she became a finalist in a contest for unpublished novelists. All finalists were encouraged to go to the conference where they would announce the winners. This was the first time Stephanie had been around other writers. "That was where I started learning the tricks of the trade," she told me. "I had always been a reader, but knew little about the craft of writing and the art of storytelling."

Becoming a finalist led Stephanie to her agent, who helped sell Stephanie's first book in 2003. It had been hard to get the attention of publishers as an independent writer, but her agent had better connections. She sold several other books on proposal within a year. Those sales gave Stephanie the confidence and the imperative she needed to leave Nike, since she now had book deadlines to meet.

Over the next few years, she sold twenty-five books to four different publishers. Stephanie used many of the skills she developed as a lawyer to manage her writing career. She reviewed her own contracts and steered her career so effectively that she didn't have to rely on her agent to negotiate with her publisher.

In 2008, she moved back to Boston from Oregon, fully occupied as a writer. She was busy and excited, until all four of her publishing relationships evaporated over the course of two months. As if this weren't stressful enough, Stephanie was getting divorced at the same time.

The pressure to find new publishers hurt her work. "I focused too much on what I could sell, and lost the magic in my writing," she admits. As a consequence, she couldn't sell anything for some time. She went into a downward spiral. Now divorced from her husband, with her daughter at home, she needed money but didn't want to go back to being a lawyer.

This was her lowest point. "When I couldn't sell any more books, people were starting to tell me that maybe I should stop writing, because I seemed to be failing at it. And if they didn't tell me, I could see they were thinking it," she says.

In 2011, Stephanie got the break she needed. Amazon had recently opened its doors to independent publishers, allowing writers to upload their books directly. With the rise of the e-book, consumers no longer depended on the physical copy that publishing houses produced. Amazon decided to let authors sell their e-books directly to consumers through its platform.

Self-publishing on Amazon allowed Stephanie to reach an entirely new audience. In fact, Stephanie made more from selling on Amazon in one year than she did in the entire eight previous years of her writing career.

Stephanie thinks she writes better without a publisher looking over her shoulder, but her previous experience with publishers gives her a competitive edge. "Some authors struggle more than I do, because they may not know when their books are ready to be published," she explains, but having worked with publishers for so long, "I know when my books are ready."

Stephanie also knows how to create more professional packaging and e-reader conversions than many other authors because of her experience working with publishers. "You have to be both creative and businesslike about writing," she says. "The more you understand how the business works, the more you can make it work for you."

Stephanie is now a nationally best-selling author of more than twenty books. She has won the Golden Heart award, issued by the Romance Writers of America, and has been nominated for its RITA award four times. She has the freedom to structure her days as she likes, which generally include writing, playing tennis, and spending time with her family. But it's mostly writing. "I work all the time now," she says, "but I love it, because I love what I do, and it makes my life rich, and that is a beautiful thing."

Stephanie's success illustrates the value of listening to your instincts and being open to new opportunities. Moving across the country to work for Nike was a great experience, but making such a big career and geographic move so suddenly might not have been feasible for someone else. Stephanie also took full advantage of the opportunity in Amazon's decision to let authors self-publish. Her success as a writer also stemmed in part from the same sense of adventure, together with talent, persistence, and the competitive edge of her publishing experience.

What I find most striking about Stephanie's path is her determination to continue writing even when most of her publishers were folding up their tents. Her tenacity, creativity, and persistence led to her eventual success as an independently published author. She now sells more books online than she did when her books were in print, and she is in total control of her writing career.

You don't need to have that kind of fan base to have a satisfying writing career. Nathaniel Stearns has integrated his work as a writer, editor, and art advisor with time at home with his children. He followed his passion for American mid-nineteenth-century folk art drawings to become an expert in that area. He writes and consults as his schedule allows, and finds more joy in that balance than he did in law. Nathaniel exemplifies the deep sense of living a good life that can come from staying true to your ideals.

Nathaniel Stearns, Art Advisor

Nathaniel Stearns is a writer, art adviser, and poet who lives with his family outside Boston. After graduating from Harvard,

Nathaniel worked for three years before pursuing a graduate degree.

Like many articulate people, Nathaniel chose law school because it seemed like the most appropriate route for someone whose strengths were more verbal than quantitative. He thought there was no downside to law school, as it would open up a range of job options. More importantly, he wanted to achieve something significant, and law school seemed like the best training ground.

While he enjoyed his law courses at Boston University, he was surprised by how little he liked practicing law. He went to work for a midsized firm, and then moved to the trusts and estates practice of one of the largest Boston firms. Although he had interesting colleagues and clients, ultimately he wasn't engaged by the work. He found it especially difficult to operate under the pressure of what seemed to him like artificially tight deadlines.

What bothered him most was the sense that he was wasting his time on something that did not resonate with him on a personal level. Nathaniel valued introspection, intuition, and the art of writing, which weren't perceived as billable qualities. He kept favorite poems and artwork in his desk drawer to look at surreptitiously as a form of stress relief. Although he was earning a good living, the salary alone wasn't rewarding enough to outweigh the anxiety and boredom he felt. He had achievement, but no sense of enduring accomplishment.

He did like writing, however, and he had always been good at it. He also enjoyed the status that being a lawyer conferred. "If you tell people at a cocktail party that you're a lawyer, you don't have to say much more to explain yourself," he says, "and that's a great thing for an introvert like me." At one of those cocktail parties, however, Nathaniel met someone who had done something different with his life every decade or so. That stayed with him. "I didn't want my obituary to end with the fact that I just practiced law," he says.

After sticking it out for a few more years, the sense that he was living someone else's life became almost unbearable. Although he's not an especially superstitious person, Nathaniel believes in signs. One day, while he was walking to work and dreading the day to come, he passed by someone handing out quotations from the Bible. Nathaniel took one, which read: "For what shall it profit a man, if he shall gain the whole world, and lose his own soul?" (Mark 8:36)

He started looking for a way out. He applied to the LLM program at the University of Cambridge in England, where he could combine his dream of studying in Cambridge with the perception of building on his law degree. He suspected he might not use the LLM, but saw it as a respectable way to ease himself out of law practice. He stayed in Cambridge for another year after receiving his degree in order to write and be with his fiancée, whom he had met there.

When he returned to Boston, he saw a career counselor who had an excellent track record of placing lawyers in non-law jobs and confirmed his natural predilection for the arts. Nathaniel followed his personal interests and pursued freelance work in the art world. He was soon editing books on naïve art and early photography. In the process, he started building the network of connections that he would draw on later in his career as a writer and an art advisor.

Nathaniel started writing articles on folk art, which had always interested him. Those articles helped him make more connections in the art world. He went on to curate an exhibition of folk art that traveled to three major institutions. He also developed relationships with a number of collectors, and now consults with them on how best to develop their personal collections. He has built a reputation as one of the foremost experts in New England on mid-nineteenth-century American folk art drawings.

The transition away from law was painful at first. The drop in income was hard to bear, as was the sense that he wasn't meeting other people's expectations of him. As an introvert, Nathaniel notes, it was especially daunting to chart his own path, but in the end, it was especially rewarding. "When my first article came out, I thought I would rather have that article with my name on it than a million dollars," he says.

When his daughters were young, Nathaniel decided to spend more time at home with them and to write less frequently. As his oldest child entered high school, however, his time for writing picked up, and he began publishing in national magazines like *Antiques*. Still, he says, "My career is completely secondary to child rearing." Parenting his daughters has also changed his views on what it takes to live the good life. It is easier to pursue your passions, he says, if you consciously value doing what you love more than maintaining a certain lifestyle or living up to some other people's expectations of what law school graduates should be doing.

If he could have done anything differently, he says, he might have spent more time looking at other ways to practice law. "I worried that somewhere there was a group of people that I would have enjoyed working with," he says, "but I never found a true mentor in my law firms, or colleagues that I connected with on a personal level." His experience as a lawyer was so jarring, however, that it soured him on the notion of working for anyone else.

Nathaniel's current career in art uses the research, writing, and editing skills he had used as a lawyer, and allows him to apply those skills to a subject he loves. To this day, however, some members of his family still find it confusing that he is no longer practicing law. To them, it may seem like a waste of his legal education. To Nathaniel, practicing law for longer would have led him down the wrong path, and further from his true self.

9

THE ENTREPRENEURS

Some of the most innovative and passionate people I have ever met are entrepreneurs, and many are former lawyers. Some, like Phil Rosenthal, start businesses that cater to the legal profession. Phil graduated from Harvard Law School after studying string theory at CalTech. He was a midlevel associate at Covington & Burling when he left to start a new kind of legal research company with his colleague Ed Walters. Their company, Fastcase, was named one of the top one hundred digital content providers in 2013, along with Google, Facebook, and Amazon, by *E-Content* magazine.

Other former lawyers create new businesses that are entirely unrelated to law, like the entrepreneurs profiled here. No matter what his business focus, every lawyer-turned-entrepreneur I have met uses his legal background to some competitive advantage. Peter Dziedzic is a great example of someone whose expertise was critical to the success of his new business, even though he had never run a business before. He drew on his experience in private equity to draft the business plan that helped get funding for skoah Boston, his award-winning spa in Boston's South End.

Peter Dziedzic, Proprietor of skoah Boston

Peter Dziedzic, a former private equity lawyer at a large Boston firm, left to open the first U.S. location of skoah, a store he had fallen in love with while on vacation in Canada. skoah Boston has won the coveted "Best of Boston" award every year since it opened and has been featured in national style magazines.

Pete didn't grow up wanting to be a lawyer. Although he intended to go to medical school, he had second thoughts during his sophomore year at Yale and decided on law instead. Pete enjoyed the business side of law and knew he wanted to join a corporate practice in the Northeast.

When he graduated from the University of Virginia Law School in 2002, however, there wasn't much deal work to be had anywhere in the country. He worked on private equity deals for Ropes and Gray, a prestigious Boston firm, for four years before transferring to Weil Gotshal.

Pete started doing the bankruptcy work that had become a big part of Weil's corporate practice. He disliked the destructive nature of the work and the arrogance of the clients he was helping to dissolve, including Lehman Brothers. The fact that taxpayers would be bearing the high cost of his firm's work for Lehman also bothered him.

Although he was then close to the point of partnership evaluation, Pete was far from sure that he wanted to make partner. "I looked at the way junior partners were treated, and how hard they worked. I saw how disrespectful the firms' clients were. I didn't feel like I was building something, as I had in my private equity practice; it was just the opposite, in fact. And I decided I didn't want that life for myself."

He had been practicing law for seven years and wasn't sure what to do next. He started looking at other options, but found nothing that appealed to him. Although he considered going in-house, he felt that being in a general counsel's practice would be like being a cog in a wheel. He wanted more autonomy than that.

In July 2009, Pete and his husband went on vacation to Vancouver. When they walked into a spa called skoah, Pete fell in love with its methods and products. He kept thinking about skoah after they returned to Boston. Pete's husband, who worked for an insurance company, encouraged him to think about starting a branch in Boston. He offered to pay the bills while Pete started the business. Pete thought that was crazy, since he had no retail experience, but he was also excited.

In August 2009, a few weeks after his vacation, he approached skoah's owners with a proposal. At the time, skoah's owners had only a few locations, all in Canada. The company was like their child, and they had to evaluate the decision to work with Pete carefully. They needed to be completely comfortable with him and his goals. But from the first conversation, it was obvious that both sides thought about things in the same way. The initial call was scheduled for fifteen minutes, but Pete and the skoah owners spent two hours on the phone. The owners agreed to consider a plan if Pete could make it work.

Pete had never started or run a business before. Although he wasn't starting entirely from scratch, as he was partnering with an existing company, he had a lot to learn. He got much of what he needed to know from the Internet, including the Small Business Association website, and a few well-chosen books.

He also spent a lot of time doing research and running numbers. He made assumptions and financial projections based on skoah's growth in Canada. He researched the company's competitors to find out what people liked and didn't like about them.

Pete was still at Weil Gotshal, but left the firm a few months later to work on the project full time. By that time, Pete had used his private equity training and his negotiation experience to work out a term sheet with skoah's owners. The term sheet included a license and distribution agreement that was exclusive in Massachusetts.

Now all he had to do was get a bank loan in 2009, in what Pete describes as "the worst market known to mankind." He approached between forty and fifty banks with his business plan. Almost all of them refused to lend to businesses that hadn't been in operation for at least two years. All but six of them rejected his application within ten minutes.

At this point, most people might have given up. Pete notes that his husband's emotional and financial support was critical. He knew how unhappy Pete had become, and he could see that working at another law firm was untenable. Pete had confidence in himself as well. "I learned at Yale that I was a capable person; that I could take chances and if things didn't work out, it wouldn't be so bad. If I hadn't gotten the financing, I would have wasted a year or two of my life and then found something else to do."

But he did get the financing. By February 2010, two banks had given Pete viable terms. Pete credits his success in part to his professional experience. "I knew what good business plans would look like because I worked on them at Ropes for years. That experience allowed me to put a plan together that would impress the banks, if they would give me a chance."

In July 2010, one year after he first saw skoah in Vancouver, Pete opened skoah Boston in the South End. Its success has been tremendous. In its first year of operation, skoah won the "Best of Boston: Facials" title by *Boston Magazine*. In September 2012, *InStyle* magazine named skoah the best place to get a facial in Boston. Pete describes this national recognition as a "huge boost" but adds that "it's nothing you can plan on." In early 2013, Pete announced skoah's expansion to two additional locations in greater Boston.

Pete has no regrets about starting his business or the time he spent practicing law. He draws on his legal experience all the time. "As a small business owner, you don't negotiate that many contracts," he notes, "but you do focus a lot on customer service." Having spent so many years in the service business of law, Pete knows a lot about what it takes to keep customers happy. His skoah clients are less demanding and more appreciative than his legal clients were. "I rarely have to deal with nasty clients," he says. "Nobody ever has a facial emergency."

Pete's family and friends have been largely supportive of his new career. Although his parents were initially concerned about his giving up the salary and security of his legal career, they applaud his transition. "My mother loves the products," he says. Most people found his pivot from lawyer to store owner so interesting that they want to see it succeed. For his part, Pete has found work he loves and a community of grateful clients.

Pete's decision to start a business with no prior experience in that area was a calculated risk. By using his private equity experience and his general analytical skills to run forecasts, however, Pete minimized the risks he and his lenders would take. Still, starting a new business is always risky to some degree. That makes it especially challenging for many lawyers. Law as a profession tends to attract the risk averse.

In addition to mitigating risk, some entrepreneurs find that their legal experience helps them develop a customer base. Valerie Beck of Chicago Chocolate Tours used her knowledge of law firm culture to tap into summer associate programs and women's initiatives at the largest Chicago law firms, bringing large customer groups to her young business and jump-starting some word of mouth publicity.

Valerie went from practicing corporate law to selling Mary Kay products to starting her own chocolate walking tour company in several cities. She manages a staff of tour guides and local directors, and partners with a number of hand-picked charities. She also makes time to mentor other women business owners and encourage their success. After leaving the law, she turned a lifelong passion for chocolate into a thriving and personally rewarding business.

Perhaps the most immediately striking thing about Valerie is her effusive, warm personality. I have known her for close to twenty years, and have always thought of her as a people person. It's hard to imagine her being happy in a traditional corporate practice. The customers on her company's chocolate walking tours, which include hot chocolate tours in the winter, are grateful that she didn't stay there.

Valerie Beck, Founder of Chicago Chocolate Walking Tours

Valerie Beck owns an expanding empire of chocolate walking tour companies. She created her business out of a passion for chocolate, which she used to consider an avocation rather than a career. When she first stepped away from the law, she didn't know how much she would enjoy being an entrepreneur, or even how to start a company. One small step led to another. This gradual progression, combined with Valerie's self-confidence and resourcefulness, led her to start Chicago Chocolate Walking Tours in 2005.

Valerie's love of chocolate began years before law school. She was unusually drawn to chocolate as a child. Her mother asked her schools to allow Valerie to drink chocolate milk because she refused to drink any other kind. During a college semester abroad in Paris, she studied chocolate more than anything else, and spent an inordinate amount of time at Debauve & Gallais. For her twentieth birthday, she led her first chocolate tour, guiding fellow students around her favorite chocolate stores in Belgium.

Like most people, Valerie didn't think chocolate would lead to a career. Her family made it clear that she should get some kind of postgraduate degree after graduating from Harvard College. She chose law. "I thought I could wear cuter outfits as a lawyer than as a doctor," she says.

She went to Harvard Law School, and hated it from the first day. She took time off to train with European law firms, returning to get her J.D. in 1996. By 1998, she had landed in the corporate practice at Winston & Strawn's Chicago office.

Law practice didn't suit her any better than law school had. "My heart was not in any aspect of my law job," she says. "I liked my relationships with my colleagues, but that was only a small part of my day. Most of the time, I was revising the Third Amended Ancillary Agreement on some project I didn't really care about." As an extrovert, she found the long, solitary hours revising documents almost unbearable. One of her most reliable coping mechanisms was good chocolate.

Her "aha!" moment came one weekend in 2000. Valerie had become a good customer at some of the best chocolate stores in Chicago. When a group of friends came to visit, Valerie decided to give them a tour. She imagined what a chocolate tour business might look like, and got 350 free business cards printed up for this business that didn't exist yet. Her friends loved the tour. The store owners she visited, whom she hadn't called in advance, loved the idea of a tour. So did the other customers in each store, who overheard Valerie talking about the tour idea. Valerie handed them each one of her new cards, moving in that moment from a fictional business to a real one.

It would be five more years before Valerie ran her chocolate tour business full time. At first, she tried to stick it out as a lawyer. She left Winston & Strawn for a smaller firm, but found the work just as stifling and the hours as long. She went in-house to Arthur Anderson, and found the culture there pervasively unethical. She wasn't surprised when the firm went under a few years later.

When she decided to leave law entirely, it wasn't for chocolate. "I became a Mary Kay director," she says. "I had been wearing the products. I loved the company. I was interested in entrepreneurship, and Mary Kay Ash was a pioneer in her field. I thought that selling Mary Kay would allow me to get my business training while working in something fun, like cosmetics."

Valerie started her chocolate walking tour company as a part-time venture. She worked out terms with her favorite stores and set up a tour website. At first, Valerie would make herself lead a tour every Saturday at 3:45. "I would show up every Saturday even when nobody had signed up in advance. I hoped for walk-ins, and if nobody showed up, I would go home," she says. "Then I started thinking about what I could do differently. I told people on my e-mail list to look for a green balloon, and I would stand outside the meeting point holding that balloon. If nobody came, I would give the balloon to a child and go home."

Although it took a while for her business to succeed, the initial drop in salary didn't bother her much. "I don't worry a lot about money, and I didn't want financial fears to hold me back from pursuing this. I didn't want my past to interfere with my future," she says.

Over time, Valerie improved her strategy. A SCORE advisor told her to think about what kind of customers she wanted. She realized that law firms were full of potential clients. She invited the biggest Chicago firms to consider her tours for their summer associate programs and women's initiatives. She reached out to the bridal market as well, and started networking with the visitor convention bureaus. Her efforts paid off. She now runs chocolate walking tours in Chicago full time, and expanded to Boston and Philadelphia in 2009. New York, she says, is next on the list.

Owning her own business fits Valerie's personality better than practicing law ever did. "I was playing against type in law school and as a lawyer," she says. She's energized by personal connections, which were scarce in her law practice. As an entrepreneur, however, she connects with people all day and every day. Much of what she loves about her work is the opportunity to nurture relationships with her team, with her customers, with the store owners, and with her company's charity partners.

"What I love about my job is working with different stakeholders," she says. "The chocolate makers are always working on some exciting new thing. My customers are the nicest people in the world, and they come to us already happy because they are thinking about and experiencing chocolate. I make a point of personally welcoming our top customers."

Running a chocolate walking tour company isn't always easy, but Valerie loves it. It's not the chocolate itself that makes the difference. It's that Valerie has a mission based on her passion rather than a job she doesn't really care about. "Every job has its up and down days," she says, "but my worst day as an entrepreneur is better than the best day I ever had as a lawyer."

While some entrepreneurs start businesses based on their personal passion, like Valerie, others start businesses for more pragmatic reasons. Christina Whelton likes biotechnology, but that wasn't her main reason for starting her own biotech placement firm. She created her business because she knew she could run it efficiently without a bricks-and-mortar space, and because it would give her total control over when and where she worked. That flexibility is invaluable to her and to her family.

Christina's experience as a lawyer has helped her at every stage of her transition, especially when her former employer decided to sue her just as her new business got off the ground.

Christina Whelton, Founder of Place Boston

Christina Whelton is a senior partner in Place Boston, the biotech placement firm that she founded in 2006 to help biotech companies staff their clinical operations. But she doesn't come to recruiting from a biotech or even a patent background.

After law school, Christina became a criminal defense attorney on Long Island. She defended her first case twenty-nine days after being admitted to the bar. She liked being at the courthouse and the pace of having several cases each day. At the same time, it was exhausting. Her clients' arraignments often went late into the night, and she would then have to get up in the morning to try another set of cases.

After six years of criminal defense work, Christina burned out. She moved over to an insurance defense firm that promised a lot of litigation, but didn't fulfill its promise. "In the six months I was there, I saw the inside of a courtroom twice," she says. Being in an office for so much of the time was unbearable. She had thrived as a criminal defense attorney in part because she didn't focus on any one case for long. Years later, Christina would be diagnosed with attention deficit disorder. At the time, however, she only knew that she couldn't stand the pace of her new practice.

Frustrated with the firm, she left law entirely. She took some time to be home with her young daughter and was out of the paid workforce for four years. While she was contemplating her next steps, she helped a friend who ran a matchmaking service. "The business was a disaster," says Christina, "I tried to figure out what was wrong with it." Troubleshooting her friend's business exposed her to a new industry and helped her get used to working again.

While she didn't like personal matchmaking per se, she did like the idea of matching people to jobs. Christina found an entry-level position in a placement firm near Boston. Because it was a commission-based job, the firm took relatively little risk in hiring her, but Christina still had to convince them that she was a good bet. Most of the job, she realized, involved selling. "I knew I would be good at sales because I sold my services over and over again when I was a lawyer," she says. "My law background makes me confident, which made it easy for me to get on the phone with people I didn't know and learn about their businesses."

To maximize her success, she taught herself about the major players in the biotech industry. Although she wasn't especially interested in science, she found it fascinating to learn about biologics and the drug development process. She also realized that biotech is a growth field, especially as the population ages.

Christina worked for the firm for eighteen months before she decided to start her own business. "I thought I could do it more efficiently," she says. After looking into the costs and considering her business's needs, she realized that she did not need a bricks-and-mortar office. Instead of spending $18,000 a month on rent, she secured a much less expensive post office box on Boston's posh Newbury Street. That gave her business the cachet of a prestigious address without the expense.

The transition from law to recruiting wasn't as hard as she expected. Both jobs require an element of persuasion. "As a criminal defense lawyer, I had to sell myself and my firm to clients. I gave the same ten-minute speech over and over again," she says. "The same is true in recruiting, although of course it's a different speech." As a recruiter, she convinces people who are usually happily employed to change jobs and join her clients instead.

The problem-solving skills she developed as a lawyer also come into play. She enjoys thinking strategically about how to help her candidates get what they want from work in a way that helps her client employers. "There is some reason why anyone might be persuaded to change jobs," she says. "There is almost always some need that is not being met. You just need to figure out what it is."

The procedural nature of recruiting, she says, is also similar to that of criminal defense. "After you've tried a lot of criminal cases, you realize that each type of case involves the same series of small steps. All DUIs are the same in that way, and drug cases are too," she says. "Recruiting works the same way." Once you master the steps of the recruiting process, she says, the positions become easier to fill.

Her law background came in handy when her former employer sued her for violation of a noncompete agreement. The firm hired some lawyers and Christina represented herself. When the court issued a temporary injunction against Christina's new firm, she had nothing to do but focus on her side of the case. She started to think about discovery requests. After she explained the scope of discovery she would be seeking from her former employers, they reconsidered their strategy. The two sides settled soon afterward.

Christina admits that some aspects of her job are repetitive, since she often has the same conversation with several different people before finding the right fit. Another downside is that candidates sometimes assume that Christina is not as intelligent or well-educated as they are. "I don't care to point out that they are wrong, but I will if they are particularly snotty," she says. "My commission is 20 percent of their salary, and I place far more than five of them a year. They can do the math."

The best thing about Christina's job, in her view, is its extreme flexibility. "My daughter is the center of my universe," she says. "Having the freedom to make my own hours and work as hard as I want to, or not at all, is critical to me." She controls her own schedule, and can go skiing with her daughter, for example, whenever she likes.

She also controls the substance of her work. Every day, Christina and her partners decide which jobs they want to fill, and therefore the people they want to talk with that day. Some days, for example, they focus on directors of clinical operations. On other days, they may work with medical writers.

Since almost all of her work is done by phone and online, she can work from anywhere in the world, as long as she adjusts to the time zone her clients are in. She rarely meets with clients or candidates in person. She can work from anywhere, so her personal travel possibilities are endless. It's a sea change from litigation, she notes, where you had to be in court when the court demanded. "I will never leave this job," she says, "and I will never leave this industry."

While Christina loves her new business, she says she "wouldn't trade her legal education for anything." Her legal training gives her a unique understanding of the business world. "As a lawyer, you understand the rules and mechanics of society differently, and that's incredibly valuable even when you're working as a 'civilian,'" she says. She encourages lawyers who are considering a different career to follow their instincts. "No matter how far you've gone down the wrong road," she says, "turn back."

Some lawyers-turned-entrepreneurs help other entrepreneurs. Mary-Alice Brady is one of them. She used her advocacy and problem-solving skills to create MosaicHub, an online community for entrepreneurs. When she practiced law, she enjoyed advising start-up companies more than the larger and better-established clients she worked with. Creating MosaicHub allowed Mary-Alice to advise those start-ups outside of a law practice, and to connect them with each other.

Mary-Alice's story illustrates the ways in which a lawyer might use the skills of creative problem solving and persuasion in a more entrepreneurial role. "I use my problem-solving skills every day as an entrepreneur," says Mary-Alice.

Entrepreneurs also have to be persuasive advocates for their own business. They have to convince potential team members to join them on the strength of their faith in the business, even when they can't offer a competitive salary. They have to persuade potential investors to fund them, which requires demonstrating that a number of unknowns are likely to work in the business's favor and that the leadership team is qualified to succeed. The advocacy skills Mary-Alice honed as a lawyer have helped her at every stage of MosaicHub's growth.

Mary-Alice Brady, Founder of MosaicHub

For Mary-Alice Brady, the founder and CEO of MosaicHub, law school seemed inevitable. Her family assumed she'd go to law school because she had always been good at arguing. After majoring in political science, and watching law shows on TV, practicing law looked like the best use of her natural talents. She went directly from Boston College to Boston College Law School, with the goal of trying cases. After spending her first summer in a small litigation firm, however, she realized that she didn't like the adversarial nature of litigation.

In her second year, a Corporations class opened her eyes to business law, which she loved. She scored a position at a large Boston firm doing general corporate representation, and stayed there for seven years. She liked being able to advise clients on a wide range of issues. As the economy changed, she found herself handling an increasing number of leveraged buyouts.

She enjoyed working with her clients, but she didn't enjoy the sense that everything she was doing was designed to maximize profits. The partners' unpredictable, time-sensitive demands also started to bother her. She would frequently get calls on a Friday saying that she needed to prepare something complex for a meeting the following Monday or Tuesday, ruining any chance of a weekend.

When Mary-Alice was two years away from partnership, she had strong reviews but concerns about staying at the firm. She wanted a closer relationship with a single company. She was also worried about what her life would look like if she stayed. The few women partners were not compelling role models. They always seemed to be struggling to find time for family. She talked with senior partners about retention issues, but their answers didn't make her feel better about the prospect of staying.

She thought about starting a consulting firm to help firms like hers improve retention and offer their attorneys career-planning help, but set the idea aside because it seemed so unattainable. "I come from a family of engineers," she says. "Nobody started their own business."

She started accepting calls from headhunters. One of those calls led to her next role, at Fidelity, which was looking for a corporate lawyer to help with business development, strategic acquisitions, and corporate governance issues. They offered her a great title—vice president and associate general counsel—and a nice salary.

What she loved most was the hours. "At first, it was hard to get used to the fact that I didn't have to check my BlackBerry after six p.m.," she says. Mary-Alice now had the time to live a fuller life. She developed deeper relationships with her friends. She began guitar lessons and took soccer.

Going in-house had its disadvantages as well. Frequent layoffs among the senior management led to people watching out more for their own interests than for their team. Although she saw the entire company as her client, she was discouraged from helping certain groups within it. She also found the work less than challenging and became increasingly bored. She started thinking about leaving Fidelity six months in, but stayed for three years.

While she was still at Fidelity, Mary-Alice told the CFO of General Catalyst, one of her former clients, that she was thinking of starting a consulting business. He offered Mary-Alice a position doing legal work that would let her pursue her consulting idea on the side. "It was a very nice safety net," she says.

General Catalyst set Mary-Alice up with an office, business cards, and a steady stream of work. Its work could have kept her busy full time, so she had to be conscientious about carving out time to create her consulting business.

As she did, she gravitated toward helping entrepreneurs. She loved their passion and dedication. She was also attracted to their creativity, and wished her own legal work allowed more room for that. She decided to focus her new business on helping entrepreneurs find answers to their most pressing questions, which often had to do with funding and finding service providers. Mary-Alice had developed a lot of expertise in this area, and enjoyed providing the answers.

In essence, Mary-Alice was working two jobs. During the day she handled legal work for General Catalyst and at night and on the weekends she worked on her business. In the early stages of her business, having the safety net of a day job allowed her to analyze the market and test products before she launched them full time. But she could only achieve so much while working on the business part time. At some point, Mary-Alice knew she would have to take the leap and focus on her new, not yet fully formed business full time.

Once she did so, the numbers started to improve dramatically. Looking back, she thinks she could have spent more time building her team while she was still at General Catalyst, but she needed to leave before her business could really take off.

Leaving took a while. "I should have left General Catalyst a year before I did," she says. Mary-Alice negotiated her departure with the company, which, unsurprisingly, wasn't eager to let such a talented person go. She agreed to stay until they could find a new GC to replace her, a process that took months longer than she expected.

Mary-Alice's business, MosaicHub, became an online community and resource center for entrepreneurs. Mary-Alice has received all kinds of accolades for her work, including being named one of the *Boston Business Journal*'s "40 under 40" in 2012, an honor awarded to "business and civic leaders who collectively represent the next wave of talent and commitment in the Boston economy."

And is she happy? "I have no regrets at all," she says, "but there are still times when I think about what I've given up." She is justly proud of having created an online community and a successful business. She points out that she saved a lot of money on business school tuition, since she has learned more about how to run a business from running a business than she would have in school. In fact, she says, people now ask her for business advice more than they ask her for legal advice.

Rebranding herself wasn't easy. It took her a long time to get over the instinct to describe herself by saying "I'm a lawyer," as she had done for thirteen years. Now, however, she says, "I'm an entrepreneur" with confidence. She has a genuine passion for what she's doing, and especially for the potential of social media, that instills that confidence.

MosaicHub's success opened new doors for Mary-Alice, but she hasn't wanted to walk through any of them yet. Many people have approached her with jobs involving senior roles in sales, management, and other areas outside of law. She is flattered by the offers, but her career goals are clear. She is committed to growing MosaicHub, and to making the most of its enormous potential and her own.

10

THE ARTISANS

For some ex-lawyers, the right professional path leads them to work with their hands. Some lawyers become professional chefs or interior designers. Others become woodworkers or jewelers. The transition from law to creative production may be the hardest kind, because in some ways it represents a shift from left-brain to right-brain thinking. It tends to invite more disbelief, and perhaps more respect, than other transitions. It also introduces an element of physical work that most lawyers never enjoy. While all of the former lawyers profiled in this section use their analytical skills to further their businesses, their working lives focus more on designing and creating than on linear thinking.

Karina Gentinetta exemplifies this use of analytic skills to further a creative venture. Karina's story appears to have a lot to do with luck, at first glance. She had the terrible luck to lose her home in Hurricane Katrina. Conversely, she had the terrific luck to sell her first pieces on Etsy to a celebrity. But on closer inspection, Karina's meteoric rise has much more to do with her innate talent, persistence, interpersonal skills, and persuasive ability, all skills she had used as a lawyer. Her experience in public relations helped, too.

Karina Gentinetta, Designer and Artist

How did Karina Gentinetta go from being a partner in a New Orleans law firm to a rising star in the interior design world in the space of three years? Part of her success is due to her incredibly high energy level, which led the *New York Times* to call her "ebullient as a fountain on hyper-spritz." But the greater part of her success is due to the skills that helped her become the "queen of summary judgment" and a partner at her law firm, including persuasion, research skills, and resourcefulness.

Karina's parents immigrated from Argentina when she was twelve. She became an academic overachiever, winning a scholarship to Tulane and graduating with honors. Although she had always been creative, her parents did not want her to major in art because they thought she wouldn't be able to support herself.

She went from her first job, as a receptionist with an advertising agency, to her second job, as its public relations director, in a matter of months. Despite her quick rise, she didn't want to stay in public relations. She called Tulane Law School and learned that the last LSAT she could take for admission the following fall was being held in two weeks. She studied nonstop and received such a high score that Tulane gave her a merit scholarship.

After law school, Karina joined the litigation practice of a New Orleans firm. Her public relations training had prepared her to write persuasively. She quickly established herself as the firm's best summary judgment motion writer. She was analytically sharp and usually found the perfect case to clinch an argument.

She loved law practice at first. It was mentally challenging and paid well. She made partner, and became pregnant soon afterward. Partnership and parenthood did not go well together. She found herself on a conference call the day after her son was born. Paralegals were sent to her house with case materials until she came back to the office six weeks later.

When she became pregnant with her daughter six months later, she kept it a secret as long as she could.

Her daughter was four months old when Hurricane Katrina hit. Karina lost her house and everything in it. She was the only partner at her firm who suffered that kind of personal loss. While the other partners were sympathetic at first, their attention was consumed by the rebuilding process. Karina had started to dislike her job when her kids were born, and now she could hardly stand to go to work. But she had little choice. Her husband lost his job as a realtor after Hurricane Katrina, and her family depended on her income.

Her emotional state spiraled downward. The firm was struggling, and Karina had proposed that the partners reduce their draw and reinvest the additional money into marketing and development. A few days later, the senior partners told her that they were taking her up on her idea and reducing her salary, and hers alone, by 75 percent. Karina resigned.

When she quit, she had no clear idea of what to do next. She spent the summer at home, "the first amazing summer I had with my kids," she says. That summer, she added paint and patina to a pair of antique French nightstands that she had purchased for about $50 each. She also restored a pair of chairs with mother-of-pearl inlay that had caught her eye in a local antiques shop. In need of cash, she posted all of them on Etsy.com. Selling on Etsy didn't require much money up front, so there was little downside if they didn't sell. But the nightstands did sell, and quickly, for $650.

She was stunned when she found out who had bought the nightstands: Courtney Love Cobain. Cobain went on to buy the two chairs for $750. "The day I made $1400 doing something I love was the day I changed careers," she says.

Emboldened by her success, Karina set her sights on the prestigious 1stdibs.com website, which attracted a much wealthier and more international clientele than Etsy and was much more difficult to get into. One of its requirements was that all dealers had to have a storefront, which Karina didn't yet have.

Karina rented space in an antiques mall that was opening nearby. Upscale buyers, including one from a store on New Orleans' posh Magazine Street, started buying her pieces. With the rent and commission she was paying on her sales, Karina soon realized that she could rent a Magazine Street storefront herself for about the same cost. Two months later, she moved into her own store. It was less than a year since she had resigned her partnership at the law firm.

Karina asked 1stdibs.com to consider her pieces for their site. When she didn't get a response, she e-mailed again and again, carefully crafting each message. She told them about her transition from law to design, and about how Hurricane Katrina had affected her. "I approached it the same way I approached a closing argument," she says. Finally, she got an encouraging response, asking her to send pictures of some pieces. Given her public relations experience, she knew how to photograph her pieces so they stood out. On the strength of those photos, 1stdibs.com allowed her to join the site.

Later that year, she was chosen as one of fifty-six out of more than twelve hundred 1stdibs.com vendors to display pieces at the site's first brick-and-mortar showroom, at the New York Design Center (1stdibs@NYDC). The showroom would charge her rent, but no utilities, and would handle her sales. It also would count as the storefront all 1stdibs.com vendors had to maintain. Karina shut down her Magazine Street store and loaded the pieces into a U-Haul truck, which her husband drove to New York.

She got other kinds of exposure as well. Karina had started a blog when the Magazine Street store opened. Within a few months, it had an international following. One reader was a woman in New York whose cottage had been featured in the *New York Times*. She asked whether she might introduce Karina to the *Times* reporter. Karina said yes.

In April 2011, the *New York Times* ran a two-page spread praising Karina's house for its exquisite style, and noting that Karina had decorated the entire house herself for under

$13,000. One photo showed part of a large abstract painting. People e-mailed Karina asking how much the painting was, and who had painted it. She responded that it wasn't for sale.

In fact, Karina had painted it herself. The day before the *New York Times* photo shoot, there was a twenty-foot blank space on her wall where a large armoire she sold had been. She bought a drop cloth from a hardware store and some black acrylic paint from a crafts store. She hung the drop cloth on her back fence and painted lines and swirls on it. "It took twenty minutes to do the whole thing, but it was a very emotional twenty minutes," Karina says. She put it on her wall to cover the blank space. "The paint was still wet when the *Times* reporters came the next day."

She painted another canvas, and hung it in her 1stdibs@ NYDC space. Two weeks later, the sales staff called to say that a customer wanted to buy it, but Karina hadn't even considered setting a price. She took the client's offer of $1,500. Her paintings have subsequently sold for much more.

The *New York Times* story led to a feature in *Southern Living* magazine, which led to a June 2012 story in *More* magazine. Her pieces have been used in the *Twilight* movies, and she has sold to celebrities including Michael Kors and Courtney Cox. She recently designed a high-end restaurant in New Orleans and was asked to design a hotel interior. She feels like she is just at the start of a new career, and she's excited. "It's only in the past few years, since giving up law, that I've started to live, really live, for the first time," she says.

Like Karina, Zoe Mohler's transition involved persistence, luck, and the savvy application of legal skills. Zoe's public relations experience helped her market her work so effectively that her jewelry was featured on the *Today Show*. Neither Zoe or Karina would have succeeded so brilliantly if they were not such talented artists, but their business savvy was invaluable.

Zoe's story has an especially compelling twist. Her company,

Three Sisters Jewelry Design, is named both for her three daughters and for her mother, who was one of three sisters and whom Zoe lost to cancer before her third child was born. Zoe developed her hand-stamped jewelry during her own cancer treatments a few years later. Her work has the kind of personal meaning for her and her customers that very few lawyers can claim.

Zoe Mohler, Proprietor of Three Sisters Jewelry Design

Zoe Mohler went to law school hoping to become a journalist. She loved to write, and one of her college journalism professors told her that many successful journalists came out of law practice. Halfway through law school, Zoe realized that her loans would be so significant that she wouldn't be able to pay them on a journalist's salary. "I thought about quitting then, but it wasn't in my nature," she says.

While she didn't relish the thought of practicing law, she felt strongly about being able to support herself. Her mother, who had been single for much of Zoe's childhood, emphasized the importance of self-reliance. Zoe had a nagging feeling that law wasn't right for her, but she wasn't about to change her plans on that basis. "I didn't understand the importance of instinct when I was twenty-four," she says. "I didn't think that happiness mattered, because I was raised to be practical about work."

She joined the transactional practice of a firm with more female attorneys than other firms, and stayed there for five years. When she became pregnant, she started to think about other fields. Even at her small firm, she knew she wouldn't be able to work as intensely once she had the baby. Latham & Watkins had a position open in the then-emerging field of law firm marketing. She got the job when she was five months pregnant.

Latham gave her a flexible schedule at first. She worked in the marketing office four days a week, and worked from home on the fifth day. She had a second child, and her mother took care of both kids while Zoe was at the office. When her children were four and two, her mother started feeling tired all the time. She was soon diagnosed with cancer and her health went rapidly downhill.

While her mother was dying, Zoe asked for some family leave. Her manager refused. Zoe quit. One week later, her mother passed away.

Zoe was devastated. She had lost her mother and, much less traumatically, had no job. After some months at home, she started thinking about how else she might contribute to the family's income. She knew that she didn't want to work for people she didn't respect again.

She had started taking night classes to improve her photography skills before she left Latham. She started doing weddings and portraits on the weekends, gaining confidence in her work and getting clients by word of mouth. Once she started promoting her photography, it turned into a business that kept her busy all weekend. Her husband watched the girls while she worked.

Two years after her mother died, Zoe herself was diagnosed with thyroid cancer. At the time, her youngest daughter was two months old. "I was terrified when I got my diagnosis," she says. She was still traumatized from losing her mother, and felt acutely how important mothers are to their daughters.

Zoe started radiation treatments. During her treatments, she was not allowed to have any contact with her three children because even casual contact would put them at risk for radiation poisoning. Perhaps the hardest part of her treatment was that she had to move out of the house completely for three weeks. She was essentially confined to one room for the duration.

While she was isolated, and thinking about family, she made keepsake jewelry for her daughters. She had researched how to make hand-stamped jewelry, and had found steel stamps online. She stamped metal discs that were personalized for each girl. "I'm a type-A person," she says, "and I like to do things with an end product. I couldn't have just sat and read for three weeks."

The treatments worked, and Zoe found herself wanting to make more of the stamped jewelry. She felt excited about creating personalized pieces, which few other jewelers were making at the time. "I have a charm bracelet I have been collecting charms for since before the girls were born," she explains. "I love the vintage, personal look of it, and I wanted to recreate that for my clients."

The jewelry business didn't go well initially. At her first trunk show, she didn't sell a single piece. "I sat in the car and cried afterward. It was a disaster," she says. Her husband, who is entrepreneurial by nature, encouraged her to take the business in a different direction. Instead of selling person to person, she decided to create her own website. She taught herself how to do that by going online after her kids went to sleep.

Her big break came unexpectedly. About three years ago, Zoe realized that her homemade website wasn't conveying the sense of professionalism that makes people feel comfortable buying jewelry online. She took the financial plunge of hiring a professional web designer to revamp her site. On the day her new website launched, a friend e-mailed her to say that the *Today Show* was doing a segment on personalized jewelry and broadcasting her website address across the screen. She got eight thousand hits that first day. "I believe in small miracles," she says.

But it wasn't entirely a miracle. The *Today Show* apparently found Three Sisters by doing a key word search for "personalized jewelry." At the time, few other companies produced the same kind of personalized jewelry that Zoe was creating, and she took advantage of that. She used the search engine optimization skills she learned at Latham to code her site so that it ranked highly during searches for "personalized jewelry" and "handstamped jewelry." If she hadn't made Three Sisters so easy to find, the *Today Show* would not have promoted her site.

"I couldn't have approached my business the way I have without the skills I used in law school," she says. She uses the analytical skills she honed there to understand her competition and adjust her position in response. Zoe has a better understanding of copyright law than most other artisans. She's more comfortable implementing and negotiating contracts than most small business owners.

Zoe also credits law school with helping her develop a sense of drive and confidence in her own abilities. She recalls the unspoken law school rule that you had to come to every class fully prepared and on top of your game. "Everything that I've done for my business, from learning how to build my own website six years ago to creating new jewelry lines, required that same kind of personal dedication," she says.

Zoe meets unhappy lawyers often. One works for her part time. Zoe urges lawyers who are thinking of changing careers to have confidence, and not to underestimate their own chances of success. "Before I started this business, I would never have expected that I could," she says. "I was thirty-eight when I started. But you never know. You can do more than you think you can. You just have to try."

Warren Brown is an entirely different kind of artisan: he bakes. His chain of bakeries, CakeLove, has several locations in and around Washington, D.C. He has had his own show on the Food Network, and appeared on *Oprah*. He has written four cookbooks so far, and speaks compellingly to kids about the importance of pursuing their passions.

Everything Warren has done, from college forward, has stemmed from his passion for solving problems. His advocacy for better sex education led him to law school. His need to find some joy and a sense of accomplishment in the face of an unsatisfying legal career led him to baking. His desire to figure out how to bake a better cake led him to CakeLove. His interest in helping people learn to cook and bake for themselves led him to write his cookbooks.

Warren isn't sure what problem he'll solve next, but he isn't lacking options. "The world has its share of problems to solve," he says. "I'm most interested in the ones that have a big impact, but which we don't really talk about."

Warren Brown, Proprietor of CakeLove

Warren Brown's first passion was advocating for better health education. After college, he taught sex education classes in Rhode Island and Los Angeles. Such classes, he thought, would be more effective if teachers had more relevant and engaging materials. He also argued for a more sensible approach to the subject, one that put more emphasis on prevention than treatment. He went to law school largely to improve his credibility as an advocate.

He studied public health law in law school, but nothing clicked for him. Law school wasn't what he expected. He thought he was supposed to write in legalese, which he didn't like. "I was a history major, and I stayed in that mentality," he says. It wasn't until he read the sample essay answers in a bar exam handbook that he realized he had been writing his own essays the wrong way throughout law school.

Practice was no more satisfying than law school had been. Warren was frustrated by the disconnect between the hard-and-fast rules law school focused on and the gray areas of the real world. He hated the bickering involved, too. It made no sense to go back and forth, negotiating with opposing counsel, when it was clear to Warren where they would end up. He had little interest in the kind of posturing he saw so many other lawyers doing, and wanted to do something different.

Warren took comfort in baking. He had always liked to cook, and had been interested in making food since he was a child. During his second year of law school, he had been in shared housing with a large communal dining space. He threw a lot of dinner parties. In his third year, he moved into a studio, which brought the dinner parties to an end. He started baking cakes instead, and bringing them to other people's parties. Baking became his refuge from the law.

He set out to learn everything he could about cake baking. He researched different types of cakes. He experimented with spices and nuts. He learned to make pastry creams and genoise. He sought out the best bakeries when he traveled, and tried to figure out what made them great. His goal was to learn how to bake from his own ideas, so that he wouldn't have to depend on other people's recipes. He had always liked detailed research projects, so baking made a great hobby. It also made him extremely popular.

A year into his baking experiments, it occurred to him that he could start his own cake business. His "aha" moment came one day in 1999, when he was walking through an airport carrying a chocolate cake he had baked from scratch. He was on his way from Washington to New York to spend a long weekend with family. Because he didn't have any professional white boxes, he covered the cake with blue plastic wrap.

As he walked through the airport, people kept coming up to him to ask about the cake. When he told people that he had baked the cake without using a mix, they were amazed. Their reaction might have had something to do with the fact that Warren is six foot three and had dreadlocks at the time.

As he waited for his family to pick him up at the airport, he realized that scratch-made cakes attracted a lot of energy. If he could build a business around that energy, he thought, that would really be something. "The idea of it moved me to tears," Warren says.

Leaving law to run a bakery didn't sound like a great idea to his friends and family. "People told me that I would regret it," he says. "They told me that making a business out of a hobby would ruin the specialness. I didn't think that would happen to me, and it didn't." Warren wanted to do something more rewarding than law had been for him. Baking was rewarding, especially when people tasted the final product. "I liked the feeling of knowing that I could make something special, fairly quickly, and lay claim to it. It gave me an accomplishment I could point to."

It would take another year for him to launch the business. He knew nothing about entrepreneurship, but he was a quick study and he had a credit card. In 2000, Warren started baking cakes professionally. In March 2002, he opened CakeLove, his cake and cupcake bakery, in Washington, D.C. The story of his career change, together with the quality of his cakes, attracted local attention. A story about him ran in the *Washington Post*. As the bakery's popularity grew, *People* magazine ran an article about CakeLove. Then the Fine Living Network did a feature, which led to the greatest break of all.

In January 2003, Warren got a call from the *Oprah Winfrey Show*. Oprah was doing a show on quarter life crises. Would he like to be on it? Of course he would. The publicity Warren got from his first *Oprah* appearance was priceless. Warren has since appeared on the *Today Show*, Martha Stewart Radio, NPR, CNN, and in the *Wall Street Journal*. He had his own show on the Food Network, *Sugar Rush,* for a few years too. There are now several CakeLove locations around the Washington, D.C., area, and CakeLove does a thriving online business.

Although he is one of the most successful bakers in the country, running the bakeries has been hard. There were months when he wasn't sure he could pay the bills or meet his payroll. He wasn't always sure who he could trust, and when he should listen to the negative criticism he received. It was especially difficult being a first-time business owner, with few mentors he could rely on day to day. At times, he wasn't sure whether he had made the right decision until well after the decision time had passed. "Not second guessing myself was hard," he says.

Warren has also written four of his own cookbooks. For him, teaching people how to bake is another form of education, not all that different from the sex education he found so engaging after college. His goal is to get people to take their health more seriously and to spend more time in the kitchen. "It's the best room in the house," he says. He's teaching his daughters to bake along with him.

11

THE ANALYSTS

Much of law practice involves analysis of cases, strategy, and legal arguments. The ex-lawyers profiled in this section are all skilled at finding, analyzing, and communicating information in a way that helps shape critical decisions. They have found a variety of ways to use their analytical skills in new and more enjoyable careers.

Meredith Benedict's current role in a health-care start-up, for example, draws on her experiences in health-care law and corporate and foundation relations. Meredith didn't plan to end up where she did. Taking some time off after leaving her firm, together with a lot of informational interviewing, led her to discover the particular specialty within development that was perfect for her. It also helped her find an institution she was passionate about supporting.

When she moved on to get another graduate degree, she wasn't sure what her next step would be. Her network led her to a role that draws on her writing skills and her intellectual passion for health-care policy. Meredith's experience, like those of the other former lawyers profiled here, shows that there are intellectually gratifying, personally fulfilling and unexpected ways to use analytical skills outside of law.

Meredith Benedict, Health Care Strategist

Unlike most lawyers, Meredith Benedict knew exactly what she wanted to focus on while she was still in law school. She got that focus by taking a leave of absence after her first year and working for a health-care consulting company. She returned to focus on health law and policy.

Although Meredith knew she was interested in health care, she felt a tension between her interests in policy and the attraction of money and prestige offered by big firms. She went to work for a big firm right after law school, believing that its health-care practice would offer a good compromise and that the skills she would learn there would complement her academic studies.

Her law firm experience was not what she expected. The hushed, sterile atmosphere of the firm made her miss the more collaborative, creative, and noisy environments where she'd thrived. The long hours spent often alone with lots of papers and files in a small office were especially hard for her. Because her firm work didn't satisfy her passion for social justice and community engagement, she sought other outlets. At the suggestion of one of the firm's partners, who also was her mentor, she joined the board of a hospice.

The turning point came one night while she was working late. She called her brother, who could hear how miserable she was. He asked her why she was putting in so many hours at a job where she was clearly unhappy. She told him that she wanted to be able to afford private school and other opportunities for her children, as their parents had. Her brother gently pointed out that she did not even have a boyfriend, let alone children, and that she had to ask herself if a firm job could ever provide the satisfaction she was looking for. Meredith realized that she had been justifying her unhappiness based on an abstraction. Six months later, she resigned the firm with no clear idea of her next step.

She spent several months living with friends in Paris thinking about what to do next. She believed that bold step of resigning should be met with equally bold creativity in exploring her options, and gave herself the freedom to think broadly. Some friends suggested she might be happy in roles that were still essentially legal, such as the counsel's office of a hospital. More conversations and some job interviews helped her see that that was not the bold change of direction she sought.

One piece of her future became clear. She felt strongly about working for an institution with a strong social justice mission and a central role in the community, although she didn't yet know what role she wanted to play within it.

As a hospice board member, Meredith had helped to hire a development professional. She started to wonder whether she would enjoy development herself. Some of her contacts had advised her that planned giving was a great spot for former lawyers. She went to a few meetings of the Planned Giving Group of New England, but didn't feel it was different enough from what she might do in the trusts and estates department of a law firm.

Someone else in development suggested corporate and foundation relations work, an area of development that involves collaborating with program staff and/or researchers to secure grant funding. Success involves both cultivating strong relationships with funders and building deep knowledge of programs or research. Fact-based advocacy that puts a program or research in a broader policy context can help make a more convincing case to a foundation funder, compared with the more emotion-based pitches that often appeal to individual donors. "The people I did informational interviews with pushed me in that direction because they thought I would fit best there," Meredith says, "and it ended up being absolutely the right role for me."

One year to the day after leaving her law firm, Meredith started a new development job at Boston Medical Center, a former city hospital whose mission is to serve all in need of care regardless of their status or ability to pay. Her new boss saw her J.D. as an asset. He was married to a lawyer who started her own nonprofit, and understood that lawyers who changed careers brought terrific skills to the table. He offered her the job on the spot, but also asked her to write a letter about why she wanted the job. "I wrote him a nine-page, single-spaced letter about why this was the perfect job for me. And it was."

Working for BMC allowed Meredith to leverage her health-care background and gave her the personal satisfaction of working for a mission-driven organization. At the same time, her legal training helped her see the big picture strategic goals while staying focused on all the detailed steps needed to reach those goals. Eventually, she became the director of her group. The opportunities to collaborate on multidisciplinary teams in proposal development and to see new services and programs established for medical center patients were some of the most rewarding results of her efforts.

But it wasn't all rosy. She took a huge salary cut to join BMC. On some of the early days, she had no idea whether she'd made a good choice. A few senior physicians questioned her repeatedly about her decision to leave law behind. "I built a team that accomplished a lot of great things for the institution and community, but eventually I hit a plateau," she says. She didn't think she wanted to move up to run a whole development office, and she didn't want to return to the law per se, but she did want to deepen her work and direct impact in the health-care field.

In 2008, seven years after she joined Boston Medical Center, Meredith started a master's degree in public health at the Harvard School of Public Health. Her program was designed for professionals with a terminal degree, including a J.D., who wanted to work in health policy or management.

This was another difficult transition point. She emerged from the intensive nine-month program exhausted and unsure of how to translate her new skills and past experience into a specific new role. In some cases, she was deemed overqualified for the positions she sought, and in others, underqualified.

A personal connection led to her next full-time move. "Someone introduced me to an entrepreneur who talked about change in health care the way I did," she says. Meredith never expected to be an entrepreneur. She found his ideas so compelling, however, that she decided to join his company, which focuses on providing innovative software solutions for health-care delivery organizations.

Her current role synthesizes everything she has done so far. Among other things, Meredith is responsible for tracking regulatory change. She then translates those regulatory drivers into sales and marketing strategy and messaging. She draws on her development skills in handling business development and marketing at health-care conferences. Her health-care experience and the communication and organization-building skills she developed at BMC allow her to talk easily about solving specific problems in the field and to help build the young company.

"Working for a start-up is like being on a roller coaster," says Meredith. "There are big highs and deep lows." She knows her even-keeled, pragmatic approach to problem solving is a good counterpoint to her visionary boss. She also knows that this is probably not her last job. "I still feel like I'm in transition," says Meredith. "I'm still trying to figure out how to pursue all the things that interest me and use all the skills I have to greatest impact."

Meredith has no regrets about leaving her law practice, although there are still days when she reflects on where she might be today had she stayed. She encourages people who are thinking of making the same transition to have the courage of their convictions. "You will run into person after person who will tell you that you are overqualified for this job or that job. People may tell you you're crazy to be making this transition. You just have to find people around you who tell you you're not. And you never know where they will come from," she says.

While Meredith's transition involved several turns and another degree, Sara Harnish took a different route to her post-law career. A conversation with a law school friend exposed Sara to a potential use for her analytical skills that she hadn't considered before. It also led to an internship in her late forties at a hospital she wouldn't have applied to on her own. Many ex-lawyers might reject the idea of an internship full stop, especially when they have been out of school for so long. For Sara, however, it was a great opportunity. Her internship provided Sara with the opening she needed to start a rewarding new career.

Sara Harnish, Non-Clinical Research Director

Sara Harnish attributes her career change to being lucky and staying friends with the right people. One of her key opportunities came from a law school friend who offered her a chance to intern at one of the country's most prestigious hospitals. Succeeding in that internship, however, was entirely Sara's doing. Her internship led to her current position as assistant director of non-clinical research at the Dana-Farber Cancer Institute.

Sara started her career as a litigator specializing in insurance defense cases. She never really liked litigation, although she was good at it. Once she had children, she knew it would be difficult to litigate part time. She couldn't be on a trial team because she had to meet the school bus before the court day ended. "I never loved it so much that it was hard to give it up," she says.

She tried a few other permutations of law. She got work as a contract lawyer, but the work wasn't substantial enough to be interesting. She set up her own practice, handling a few small corporate matters and divorces, and discovered that she prefers being in an office to working alone. She also realized that she didn't like business development, a key skill for solo practitioners.

When she was forty-three, Sara stopped practicing altogether. She threw herself into volunteer work with her kids' school and the town zoning board. When Sara thought about her ideal job, she thought about Nina Totenberg's coverage of the Supreme Court for NPR. She liked the idea of being inside an institution, analyzing its developments without having to make the major decisions herself.

Out of the blue, one of Sara's law school friends, Michele, e-mailed to say that she was moving to Boston for a new job. Michele had moved to Maryland after law school, and she and Sara had stayed in touch through e-mail and holiday letters.

When Michele arrived in Boston, the two went out for dinner. Michele asked Sara what she wanted to do next. Sara didn't know. Her only certainty was that she didn't want to litigate or take any other job where people fought each other all day. To Sara's surprise, Michele asked her whether she had any interest in Institutional Review Boards (IRBs). Sara had never heard of them. Michele explained that, since the 1990s, any institution that gets federal funding has had to undergo an IRB review. She was moving to Boston to oversee the IRB office at Dana-Farber Cancer Institute, which oversees the cancer-related research of all Dana-Farber/Harvard Cancer Center institutions. She offered Sara the chance to volunteer in the office.

Sara was forty-eight when she started her internship. It had been five years since she had practiced law, and she started at the ground level. For the first two weeks, she worked part time, for free. After two weeks, she was paid a small amount as a consultant. After a month, she was working forty hours a week and one year later she was a full-time employee.

"I was terrified," she says. Her computer skills were rusty. She was a Mac person working in an office full of PCs. What was more, most of the communication about patient data had to be encrypted because of HIPAA concerns. "I had nightmares that I had attached the wrong document to an e-mail," she says.

Although the technology was daunting, the cancer center's mission grabbed her. She loved the fact that everyone was focused on the same goal of curing cancer. It reminded her of what to her the best part of law practice had been: the sense that everyone was working together to solve a problem. It was more collaborative than a law firm, and there were no billable hour requirements.

Starting a new career in her late forties had its advantages, too. "Being older, I wasn't as easily intimidated by the hotshots around the hospital," she says. The complexities of the research review process didn't bother her at all. Her experience, together with her legal training, had taught her that nothing is black and white.

Sara learned everything she knows about her job by jumping in. It took her a few years to feel truly comfortable with the work, she says, but her confidence has grown over time. "It was like being in a foreign country where you speak a little of the language, and you need to get your family around safely," she explains. From time to time, she still feels a bit on edge. "I will never understand genome sequencing the way scientists do," she says.

Sara worked her way up to her current role as assistant director of non-clinical research. Part of her job involves facilitating meetings that bring together oncologists, nurses, and community members to review potential treatment protocols and informed consent forms. Sara runs more than fifty such meetings every year. Another part of her job involves reviewing the informed consent documents to make sure that they are both comprehensive and, importantly, easy for patients to understand. She also reviews the simpler treatment protocols, the ones that use standardized surveys or don't require the collection of any confidential health data.

Sara considers herself lucky both that she stayed friends with Michele and that she was able to do a short-term internship for very little pay. Otherwise, she believes she wouldn't have had the courage to apply for a position at Dana-Farber, one of the most highly rated medical centers in the country, with so little direct experience. She also suspects that she wouldn't have gotten the internship without that personal connection. In fact, she wouldn't have known that that kind of work existed had Michele not told her about it.

While her friend's influence helped her learn about the opening, the skills she had developed as a lawyer were key to her success. She draws on her legal experience when it comes to finding a solution that works for all parties. Some of the meetings she runs remind her of pretrial conferences, in that everyone is working on finding the right solution among a number of different options. Unlike pretrial conferences, they often have an ethical overlay, which Sara appreciates.

Sara's work also gives her the opportunity to solve problems, something she has always enjoyed. Helping patients who have had a bad experience get a better result is another part of her work, and draws on her problem-solving skills. She finds it more gratifying to solve those kinds of problems—of literally life and death—than the problems of large corporate clients, which usually involve making more money.

Sara still thinks of herself as a lawyer. "But I went on retired status just last year," she laughs.

One of my favorite aspects of Sara's story is that she built a new career in an unlikely setting. Many lawyers wouldn't think of applying to work in a hospital, at least outside of the counsel's office. It can be especially hard to approach an institution that prizes an entirely different kind of graduate study. Even so, ex-lawyers can work in hospitals in a variety of ways. Like most big institutions, hospitals value communication skills. Former lawyers can do well in hospital development, risk management, patient advocacy, and a number of other niches. Because lawyers are often good at interpreting and analyzing information, they may adapt particularly well to the IRB practice, as Sara has.

Another way to use analytical skills is to become a recruiter. The only recruiters most lawyers encounter are those who help place them in their firms or call them with better offers. Alison Ranney left law to become a different kind of recruiter, working with nonprofit institutions to help find their next leaders. Collaborating with the institutions and the key decision makers within them requires the kind of interpersonal skills that she once used to counsel clients as a lawyer. She manages multiple high-level searches at the same time, as a lawyer might manage multiple cases. In her current role, Alison helps provide leadership to some of the country's most important cultural institutions and universities. Her work is entirely collaborative and constructive. Most importantly, it is work she loves.

Alison P. Ranney, Senior Recruiter

Alison Ranney is a Chicago native. Her father is a respected member of Chicago's business, legal, and civic community. She graduated from the University of Chicago Law School, and joined the Chicago office of a large firm afterward. But it wasn't until she left the practice of law and moved away from Chicago that she was able to redefine her skills and move toward the recruiting career she finds much more rewarding than law.

Alison had a suspicion that she would not be a career attorney even before she applied to the University of Chicago, where she received a J.D. and an MBA. Although she hadn't originally intended to join a large law firm, those firms recruited aggressively on campus. At the same time, finding an unconventional business or legal role was harder than she expected. If she was going to join a traditional firm, she thought, she might as well get the credibility that comes with time spent at the best of them. She joined the Chicago office of Skadden, Arps, Slate, Meagher & Flom.

She enjoyed consulting with her clients and learning from the partners. As much as she admired the Skadden lawyers, she found the management style that pervaded the firm difficult. For example, it was common practice to assign projects internally at six p.m. that were due the next morning, rather than giving the associates notice of the project earlier in the day. The firm's policy was to pay for a taxi if an associate had to work after eight p.m. In one year, she remembers taking the subway home only once.

After a few years, she left Skadden, expecting that her MBA would help her find a business job. She was unprepared for the general resistance she faced from recruiters. Because of her law firm experience, she didn't fit the mold of a traditional business candidate. Many recruiters appeared to have a bias against lawyers, even those with joint MBA degrees. "I developed a real distaste for recruiters around this time," she says.

She was ready for a major change, but she felt stuck. She couldn't get recruiters to see past her law degree, and she didn't want to continue to practice law.

"What enabled me to take the next step was moving out of Chicago," she says. She and her new husband decided to move to Seattle, where they liked the entrepreneurial vibe and energy. Moving to a new location helped her refocus. "I started asking myself, 'What can I do that is interesting in Seattle?' instead of 'What can I do apart from law in Chicago?'"

In Seattle, Alison joined AT&T Wireless. AT&T was initially interested in Alison as a legal candidate. She stuck to her goal of working on the business side, and the AT&T executives agreed to place her there instead. When she explained the switch to the recruiters after the fact, they told her that they would never have been able to place her in the business role directly, given her legal background.

When Alison and her husband started a family, she wanted to return to Chicago. She missed the speed and camaraderie of the business community downtown. After some time consulting in the suburbs, she realized she was happiest when she was involved in Chicago's downtown business community. As she interviewed with search firms in Chicago, recruiters asked whether she had any interest in—well, recruiting.

"My husband and my friends thought it made perfect sense," Alison says. She liked working with people. She liked to make introductions, and had been connecting people for years. Why not try it as a profession? Although her negative experience with recruiters made her resistant at first, she quickly saw the logic.

Alison joined the Chicago office of Russell Reynolds Associates, a search firm with offices in forty countries. She is now a senior recruiter focused exclusively on searches in the nonprofit and education sectors. Her placements have included the director of the MacArthur Foundation's Fellows Program, the dean of Northwestern Law School, and the director of the Cantor Arts Center at Stanford, among others.

There is a lot to love in her work. She describes her colleagues as "high powered, funny, smart, and driven." Her clients hire her to run a disciplined search process and create a slate of top-quality candidates. At this level of search, the candidates are almost invariably already in senior roles elsewhere.

Recruiting requires a special ability to understand the clients as well as the potential candidates. In working with her clients and candidates to find the right fit, she facilitates a lot of meetings. She spends a lot of time helping clients define the qualities they are looking for. Her expertise helps inform the conversation. She and her colleagues then conduct a worldwide search for candidates with those qualities and a potential interest in the position. When the client has decided who they want to hire, she helps them extend and negotiate the offer.

She works on several searches at any one time, all of which are in different stages, so her days are varied. "It's a really fun job," she says.

Before she began her work with Russell Reynolds Associates, she doubted the rumors that recruiting was a difficult field. Now, she says, "I think it's even harder than people told me it would be." The challenge lies in dealing with two high-powered constituencies, the clients and the candidates, simultaneously. She also works with clients who may have internally diverse agendas. Although the board chair of a museum and the museum's president may have the same ultimate goal, for example, they may have different ideas about how to reach it.

Being an ex-lawyer, particularly an ex-Skadden lawyer, is an asset to her career. "That gives me even more credibility than my MBA," she says. Her clients are generally impressed with her law degree, which is more unusual in her field than a business degree. "They point to it as one of the reasons that I'm good at my job," she says. "They mention it so often that I can tell it's important to them."

Alison thinks that many former lawyers have the potential to be great recruiters, and notes that a senior member of her firm is another former lawyer. Her work as a recruiter is similar to her legal work in many ways. Both roles are client driven and project based. Both require intense collaboration with senior-level clients, who trust and rely on Alison's judgment. As a recruiter, Alison's clients tend to be the boards of directors of universities or nonprofits, or high-level executives within those institutions. The part of law Alison enjoyed most was working with clients, and client collaboration is a major part of her current work.

The differences between recruiting and law, however, underscore why Alison prefers recruiting. Rather than reviewing documents, Alison works with clients to assess who can bring the right combination of leadership skills and experience to advance their goals. Recruiting is a better match for her skills and preferences, including her interpersonal skills, than law was. "I'm a people person," she says. "As a recruiter, I get to work with different people every day."

Although Alison found it difficult to leave law at first, she advises other lawyers that their next move doesn't have to be their last. Her own path from law to recruiting was nonlinear, but she might not have ended up in such a satisfying career without those turns in the road. "Being nonlinear about your career could end up being the best thing for you," she says.

Christopher Mirabile is one of those people with enough energy to have several high-powered careers all at once. It would be exhausting to talk with him if he were not so nice at the same time. His great passions are start-ups and technology, and his current role as the leader of an angel investor network allows him to focus on those passions full time.

His transition from law firm to in-house counsel, and then up the ranks to general counsel and chief financial officer, was something of a roller-coaster ride. He got off in late 2008, at just the right time. Taking time to reflect on what he had found most rewarding and what he was truly good at helped him figure out what to do next. Being open to new possibilities, however, was key to finding the world of angel investing where he now feels so at home.

Christopher Mirabile, Angel Network Leader

Christopher Mirabile started an angel investor network after a legal career that featured one star turn after another. After his company was sold in 2008, he realized that he had been making decisions based on the options in front of him rather than the passion inside him. His talent and drive translated well into his new career co-managing Launchpad, one of the top five angel investor networks in the country.

Christopher went to law school after being a management consultant with what is now PricewaterhouseCoopers.
Although he scored higher on the GMAT than the LSAT, he had
no interest in the paths he saw people taking after business
school. "In retrospect," he says, "I would have loved to be an
entrepreneur, but I had no compelling ideas, no idea how to do
it, and no capital." While he was thinking about his options, he
read that a remarkable number of Fortune 500 CEOs had come
up through the legal side. That clinched his decision to go to
law school.

Christopher started having doubts about being a lawyer
while he was still in school. The more he learned about the
realities of law practice from friends in firms, the less he
wanted to do it. He accepted an offer at Testa, Hurwitz &
Thibeault, a Boston firm which, at the time, had a booming
corporate practice doing a large number of IPOs, venture capital fund formations, and M&A work.

Testa was a heady place to be in the mid-1990s, when Christopher graduated from law school. The firm believed in trial
by fire, and gave junior associates a tremendous amount of
responsibility without much mentoring or guidance. From the
beginning, Christopher felt more of a kinship with the entrepreneurs who hired the firm than the partners. The law firm
felt too far removed from the energy of the business world his
clients lived in and which he found truly exciting.

After taking a software company public, Christopher got the
chance to join the company in-house. He went without hesitation. So much of his firm work had been wrapped up in that
one client that it was a relatively easy transition. "It was just a
matter of scooping up the surface of my desk and moving it all
over to my new office," he says.

Christopher loved his new role from the first day. He found
the variety of people he worked with energizing. He was in the
midst of business instead of on the periphery. "It was like the
difference between reporting on foreign policy from a cubicle

and being embedded with the troops," he says. "You learn from your mistakes very quickly, because you are the one who has to fix them."

His new role capitalized on his deal-making skills. He negotiated agreements all the time, completing between thirty-five and fifty deals every quarter. He completed a $3.6 million software license deal with Goldman Sachs, on his company's basic license terms, in two weeks.

Christopher worked constantly, and was soon promoted up the ranks of the growing international company. He became the general counsel in his mid-thirties. His job required travel to Europe on an almost monthly basis, at a time when he had two small children at home. Ultimately, he became the company's chief financial officer, with nearly a hundred people reporting to him.

After a semi-hostile takeover offer, the company went through a year-long auction bidding process so complex that the prospectus ran to nearly three hundred pages. The company was sold on September 12, 2008, the day before their bankers, Lehman Brothers, went bankrupt. With the economy in free fall, and feeling like he had narrowly escaped from a burning building, Christopher was ready for some time off.

Once he stepped away from work, Christopher realized that with each promotion he had accepted, he had moved further away from the technology, strategy, and innovation that he loved. At the same time, he had sacrificed family time he could never get back. "I felt like I missed the fourth and fifth years of my daughter's life and the seventh and eighth years of my son's life doing things which, in the long run, I didn't particularly care about," he says.

Christopher got as much input as he could on what to do next. He took personality tests. He did a lot of networking, asking open-ended questions in every conversation. He pulled out the 360-degree reviews he had received at his last job, and thought about what they reflected. He asked himself the three questions he now urges every entrepreneur to ask:

1. What do I know?
2. Whom do I know?
3. What do I have (to offer)?

He spent almost a year thinking about the answers. During that time, a friend encouraged him to think about angel investing with some of the capital he had acquired. He started investing on his own, but quickly saw that it was easier to do due diligence on a start-up as part of a group. He looked at many of Boston's angel networks, each of which has a different vibe. One group he visited was Launchpad. Its leader, Hambleton (Ham) Lord, became one of his most valued mentors.

"I was fascinated by the innovation economy," Christopher says. He realized that his own skills and interests dovetailed with the angel community. He knew an increasing number of investors and business advisers who could work together to help promising entrepreneurs succeed. He was good at mentoring and building consensus in a consortium. His training and temperament helped him excel at recognizing patterns and synthesizing a great deal of information quickly. He knew he would be able to run an angel group that leveraged its members' skills to do effective due diligence and make sound investments.

"It gradually became obvious to me that this was where I should be," he says. "And then it was just a matter of working hard to reorganize my life around this calling."

Rather than joining one of the networks he had visited, Christopher decided to start his own. In 2009, he created Race Point Capital Group. He worked intensely on it for several months, knowing that it would need to be exceptionally well formed from the launch to get credibility in the crowded

Boston angel group market. Twenty investors joined right away, and Christopher found himself dealing with the rapidly compounding diligence and deal process resulting from seeing four companies every month.

He went to experienced angel group leaders for advice. While some might have felt threatened by Race Point, Ham Lord felt there was room in the market for a more dynamic new group. He had also been looking for help. After exploring the alternatives, Ham and Christopher decided to merge Race Point into Launchpad.

Two years later, Launchpad was declared one of the top five most active angel networks in the country in terms of both deal flow and dollars invested. Its wait list for membership can be several months long. "What had been a hobby or exploratory diversion at first has now become more fun and consuming than I ever thought possible," says Christopher.

Christopher advises lawyers to be entrepreneurial about their own lives. "Lawyers tend to be goal oriented and good at deferring gratification, but not as good at listening to or following their instincts," he observes. "It's easy to lose the ability to hear what your heart wants." His own experience illustrates how easy it can be to get off track—especially when the world rewards you so handsomely for it—and how immensely gratifying it can be to reconnect with what you love.

12

THE PROFESSORS

The love of research and writing that drives so many people to law school can also fuel successful careers in academia. Some ex-lawyers become schoolteachers. Bella Wong, a school superintendent, left a career in regulatory and banking law to get a master's degree in education. She taught science in suburban high schools for years and helped lead a teacher's union before working her way up to school administration.

Other ex-lawyers become university professors. While teaching in law schools may seem like the easiest transition into academia, it is an intensely competitive job market. For most law faculty appointments, the hiring process is governed by the Association of American Law Schools (AALS) and culminates in the annual Faculty Recruitment Conference in Washington, D.C. The most successful candidates have a track record of published research, and may interview with a hundred law schools before getting a single offer.

There are many ways to teach outside of the AALS process, many of which may be more attractive than re-immersion in legal theory. One way is to teach legal writing and other professional skills, like Katrina Lee, a former law partner who now teaches at Moritz College of Law in Columbus, Ohio. Another is to teach what you know outside of law. Deb Volberg Pagnotta, for example, became a communications professor after more than a decade of experience in corporate training and diversity education.

Teaching positions are notoriously hard to secure, however. While the competition for these openings is intense in most fields, the ability to bring your practical knowledge to bear in the classroom can give you a significant advantage over less experienced candidates.

Perhaps the most difficult transitions are the ones that involve an entirely new doctorate, like that of Liz Gorman, who teaches sociology at the University of Virginia. Liz didn't realize how much she enjoyed sociology until she had left law practice. Leaving gave her the time and space she needed to consider what would be genuinely fulfilling. She went back to Harvard for her master's and doctorate degrees in sociology, happily surprised by the differences between law practice and academia. Her legal experience, however, continues to inform her career. One of her academic papers surveys research on women in the legal profession.

Liz Gorman, Sociology Professor

Liz Gorman became a tenured sociology professor at the University of Virginia after spending time at some of the country's most prestigious schools and a top-rate law firm. But she didn't want to be a lawyer because of the status it confers. In fact, the hierarchy of traditional law firms was one of the reasons she left.

After graduating from Harvard, Liz chose law school because, like so many other liberal arts graduates, she didn't want to go to medical school and law school seemed like the next best option. Although her father had been a lawyer, Liz knew little about what the practice of law was like. "My father didn't push me to go to law school, but I knew it was something he would approve of," she told me.

She liked a lot about law school, especially legal analysis. "I liked identifying general principles and extrapolating from them to the case at hand, and I was good at it," she says. "What I didn't like was the hierarchy, where the very smartest people who got the best grades were at the top. It bothered me that status was based on a single trait of these very complex people." One classmate who didn't do well in school went on to become a senator, while her top-ranked classmate had a relatively undistinguished career.

After clerking, Liz joined a prestigious firm in Washington, D.C. While she liked the firm, she didn't like its close relationship with government work. "I couldn't see myself specializing in any one government agency or being an antitrust litigator, and those were my main choices," she says.

After two years in Washington, Liz made what she calls "the single most reckless decision of my life" and moved to New York. She joined the litigation practice of a Wall Street firm, and stayed there for three years before she stopped practicing law altogether. "I had gone to New York thinking that the problem was D.C.," she explains. Then she thought the problem might be litigation. Her New York firm let her switch into the corporate practice as a fourth-year associate. The transition was more difficult than she anticipated. The firm expected her to function at the fourth-year level even though she lacked the experience other fourth-year corporate associates had. She was still unhappy.

Something else was missing from her legal career: a sense of purpose. "At my Washington firm, I felt that most cases arguably had some national significance; for example, I got to work on a brief submitted to the Supreme Court. In New York, it was all about money. It took my breath away to see these incredibly smart and highly educated people spending a hundred hours a week figuring out whether one or another corporation could get a little more money."

Although she considered other options in law, nothing seemed like an improvement. She knew people who had left her firm for a smaller one, but they didn't seem any happier. In fact, they seemed to have more insecurity because the continued existence of their firms was less certain.

Just as Liz was concluding that she had run out of options in the legal profession, she met and, a few months later, married her husband. His emotional and financial support made it easier for her to finally take off the "golden handcuffs" of big firm practice. Ironically, some of the senior partners approved of her apparent departure to get married as the natural course for a young woman.

Liz took some time to clear her head and do the kind of comprehensive self-assessment she now wishes she had done in college. She read *What Color Is Your Parachute?*, and worked through the book's exercises. That led her to realize both that she had an academic bent and that she was most interested in the social sciences.

"I hadn't studied social science in college," she notes. "My parents had given me the idea that they were not 'serious' areas." But Liz gravitated toward the social science section of bookstores. She wanted to read and talk about social sciences, and knew it would hold her interest. "In certain law school classes, we would talk about how law had changed in response to societal changes. I always felt the societal changes were more interesting than the legal ones," she said.

Auditing classes at Columbia helped Liz narrow her interests to sociology. She had been out of the law firm for less than a year when she decided to apply to graduate school in sociology. She found she could still apply to NYU for the following fall, although she had missed some other schools' deadlines. After starting at NYU, she applied to some of those other schools. She got into Harvard, her top choice. Her family moved to Boston so she could join the PhD program.

"The hardest thing about going back to school was restarting the learning curve," she says. For the previous ten years, Liz had been a professional with a certain amount of autonomy. Now, she was studying unfamiliar subjects, like advanced statistics, and learning about theorists she had never read before. It wasn't easy to go back to knowing little about her field, but she was so excited about her studies that she wasn't overly concerned.

Liz loved academia from the start. It was more relaxed than the law firm world, with a far more subtle hierarchy. At her old firm, she noted, "It was clear that the firm would rather have you spend six hours trying to solve a problem on your own than take up two precious minutes of the partners' time." The academic world, she found, was just the opposite. Her new colleagues went out of their way to be collegial and inclusive.

After getting her doctorate, Liz joined the faculty at the University of Virginia, commuting on the weekends to her family in Boston. She was on the tenure track, but stopped the clock when she and her husband adopted each of their children. She got tenure, and is now an associate professor.

Liz advises unhappy lawyers to make a move as soon as they know they're unhappy, and not to wait. When she was practicing law in New York, she sometimes felt as though she were in *Invasion of the Body Snatchers*. She barely recognized the person she was during the day at the firm, but she would get herself back at night. "If your job affects you like that," she says, "listen to that voice and take some action. You don't want to wake up at seventy-five and feel bad about what you did with your life."

While Liz followed the traditional academic route of getting a doctorate in her subject before becoming a professor, Deb Volberg Pagnotta took an entirely different path to her professorship. She discovered how much she loved teaching when she created a series of training seminars on diversity. As a communications professor at Iona College, Deb teaches what she has practiced for more than a decade. The turns in her legal career provided the perfect training for the subjects she now teaches.

Deb Volberg Pagnotta, Communications Professor

Deb Volberg Pagnotta grew up in exactly the kind of environment that you'd think would lead to an interest in diversity. Born in the United States, she spent large parts of her childhood in Europe and Africa. Her daughter is Chinese. But Deb's transition from government lawyer to diversity consultant to communications professor was wholly unpredictable.

Deb went to law school because she was interested in social justice. Clarence Darrow was one of her first heroes. There was little question that she would get another degree after studying anthropology at Brandeis. In her family, college was just a precursor. "If you didn't have a graduate degree in our family, it was like you didn't exist," she says. She was good at arguing, and she wanted to change the world. Law school seemed like the best way to do that.

From her first day of law school at Hastings College of the Law, Deb realized that most of her classmates didn't share her view of law as a force for good. She found the first-year courses dry and technical. She doubted her choice until she took a seminar on environmental law, when she started to see how she might use law to further her original goals. She also liked moot court, and found that she was good at thinking fast on her feet. She enjoyed the feeling of being an advocate.

Law practice, however, wasn't what she expected. She went to work for a sole practitioner, but was disturbed by his questionable ethics and left after less than a year. She then went to a mid-sized firm. A self-described "hippie," she didn't understand the law firm hierarchies at first. But she adjusted and learned as much as she could from other attorneys. Although she liked most of her colleagues, she never felt that she quite fit in. She was one of two women there, and the youngest. After a few years, she could no longer stand working for the senior partner. His management style involved calling Deb "Sweet Lips" in front of clients and screaming at her when the clients had gone. "I cried every day," she says.

Deb then moved to the New York State Attorney General's office. One of her first responsibilities, as a young female lawyer, was to defend the corrections officers at Attica in the wake of some high-profile prison riots. Spending much of her time with the corrections officers, and frustrated by the apparent disparities in the courtroom, she decided to teach them how to run a procedurally sound hearing. In doing so, she found that she enjoyed the training process.

Her work at the AG's office was so well received that she soon had a number of new job opportunities. Mindful of how much she had liked her environmental law class in law school, she moved to the New York State Department of Environmental Conservation.

This, she says, was like finding family. She loved going out into the community and talking with people about local environmental issues. She excelled at making connections, which led to productive conversations. As she accepted promotion after promotion, educating the public became her favorite part of her work. She found creative ways to expand that educational function, including doing a weekly radio show and writing a column for the local newspaper.

One of Deb's tasks as Director of Legal Affairs at the Department of Environmental Conservation was to diversify the counsel's office. When she joined the agency, the vast majority of its attorneys were Caucasian. Over the course of two years, Deb led a diversity effort that resulted in eight new attorneys of color joining the office.

Her government work ended when a Republican governor took office and downsized the agency. Soon after the regime change, Deb found herself with twenty-four hours to clean out her own office. She advised the new administration not to lay off all eight attorneys of color, but her advice was not well received. Infuriated at the way she and her colleagues had been treated, Deb sued the new governor and lost. She decided to start her own practice, but first she had to change focus. Although she had years of experience in environmental affairs, she couldn't litigate many of the key issues because she had worked on the government side. Her unsuccessful lawsuit and the resulting publicity didn't help matters.

She turned instead to employment law. A friend offered to rent her some space in New York City and Deb moved her practice there. One of her first initiatives was developing a sexual harassment training program. The training program filled a popular need. At the time, Anita Hill was doing battle with Clarence Thomas, and sexual harassment training became practically obligatory for many employers. Deb noticed that she enjoyed training more than most other things she had done as a lawyer. She set up shop as a harassment and diversity trainer in 1999. Her company, Interfacet, offered diversity training just at the time when many corporations were starting to realize its benefits. Her experience diversifying the attorney pool at the Department of Environmental Conservation formed part of the basis for her program. She balanced her training work with some legal representation of clients. "Doing both kinds of work helped to keep me grounded," she says.

After a few years, however, Deb's priorities changed. When Deb and her husband adopted a daughter from China in 2001, she scaled back her training schedule so that she could spend more time with her daughter. In 2006, Pace University asked Deb to run the emerging New Directions program for lawyers returning to work. She saw it as another form of training. She oversaw a successful launch of the program, which exceeded all expectations Pace had for it. In 2008, however, her life took another turn when she contracted Lyme disease, which sapped her energy. She resigned from Pace, realizing that there was only so much she could balance while she recuperated.

In 2009, her diversity training came back into focus. Deb collaborated with a technologically savvy colleague to create diversi-tyDNA, a phone app that launched with great success in 2010. It evolved into a full-fledged interactive web app that allows users to compare and explore the differences in their backgrounds that can affect their communication styles. It also helps users create strategies for more effective collaboration within their organization. In 2009, Iona College asked Deb to teach a course on communications to college students. Deb started teaching occasionally, as an adjunct, and found that she loved teaching. In 2012, she became a full-time professor. She teaches communications advocacy and technology as well as courses on interpersonal and intercultural communication that use diversityDNA.

Deb enjoys teaching now for many of the same reasons she enjoyed developing training programs years ago. It's interactive, so no two sessions are the same. It lets her engage with a wide range of people and help them in the process. And it capitalizes on the interpersonal and communications skills she has honed throughout her career.

One thread running throughout Deb's career is a passion for helping people work better together. This is apparent in her work with prison guards and her community outreach for the environmental bureau. Her work on diversity training and her development of the diversityDNA app may also stem in part from a desire to help people understand each other better. In a way, teaching communications couldn't be a more fitting vocation, but it's not something she or anyone else would have expected when her career began.

Katrina Lee's transition into teaching wasn't something she expected either. A move from California to Ohio catalyzed her move from law partner to legal writing professor. She liked being a lawyer and she loves being a law professor.

The joy Katrina finds in teaching makes perfect sense when you look at what she gravitated toward in private practice. At her firm, she had chaired the recruiting committee. She started running the summer associate program as a mid-level associate, and continued to do so as a partner, years after she could have handed it off to someone more junior. In other words, she had taken on the administrative roles that allowed her to work most closely with law students and young lawyers. She also enjoyed producing briefs, and her skills as a writer and editor were admired throughout the firm and among her co-counsel, something I know from being one of them.

Katrina now has few of the administrative duties that she had disliked at her law firm. As a partner, she was often involved in dry institutional issues, like managing conflicts of interest and reviewing associates' billing records, which she tolerated as necessary parts of her job. As a clinical professor, she is assigned to committees, but her main job is to teach and mentor students. Teaching allows Katrina to focus on the parts of law practice she liked most—mentoring, writing, and editing—and to impart those skills to a new generation of lawyers.

Katrina Lee, Clinical Law Professor

Katrina Lee was, by any measure, phenomenally successful in private practice. She was promoted to equity partner in her seventh year as an associate, one of the youngest partners in her firm's history to achieve that distinction. She was also the firm's first Asian American female partner. Her commercial litigation career was stellar. In 2003, her trial team scored a $383 million jury verdict, one of the largest in the country that year, on an insurance recovery action. She was a partner for six years before she resigned, with no definite plans for a different job, much less a new career. She had plans only to stay home with her two children, then aged nine months and three years.

About a year after she resigned from her firm, Katrina started again, as a law professor at Moritz College of Law at The Ohio State University, one of the top forty law schools in the country. On her first day, Katrina stood in front of a class of eighteen students, who were nervous because it was their first week of law school. Katrina guesses that, in spite of her years of experience arguing in court and months of preparation, she was more nervous than they were.

Katrina never thought she would leave the San Francisco area, where she grew up. She went to college and law school in Berkeley. She joined an old, established San Francisco law firm after graduation. Her family all lived in the Bay Area—except for her husband, a professor at The Ohio State University.

At first, Katrina and her husband made things work long distance, with Katrina litigating in San Francisco and visiting her husband in Ohio every few weeks. She was back in court four days after getting married in 2006 on picturesque Treasure Island in San Francisco. Even after she became pregnant with her first child, she worked from her office in San Francisco. She got on the plane to Ohio only ten days before her first daughter was born, in 2007.

After two years of commuting between San Francisco and Columbus, with one child in tow and then two, Katrina officially resigned. Spending a year at home with her daughters was the toughest part of her transition.

"Being a mom with two kids was harder than anything I had done as a lawyer," she says. "I had heard that from friends, but I didn't really believe it until I did it myself." The most difficult days brought her to tears. "I had had some sleepless nights as a lawyer, but I can't remember feeling like that before," she says. Katrina soon realized that she wanted to go back to work. Before she knew exactly what she would do, she knew at a minimum that she wanted a work space outside of the house.

Katrina thought long and hard about going to a law firm in Columbus. In San Francisco, where she had been building client relationships for more than a decade, she had developed a book of business and was on her way to being a rainmaker. For the most part, that book wasn't portable. Developing new business from scratch in Ohio would have taken more time, including occasional nights, than she wanted to put into a new venture, especially with two young daughters at home.

With that in mind, Katrina looked for opportunities to use her skills in a different context. She was especially interested in teaching at Moritz, the top-ranked law school in Ohio. Her husband teaches in the same university system, and she generally thought of it as a good employer. Moritz features a strong legal writing program, and in 2010, it had an opening.

Katrina competed with candidates from all over the country for the clinical position. Although she had no prior teaching experience, her twelve years of private practice and mentoring experience set her up perfectly for the job, and she got it. She started preparing for classes in the summer of 2011. "That first summer, I felt this nice sense of balance that I hadn't had in quite a while," she says. "I had a professional space away from the house, where I could work on preparing for my first semester teaching legal analysis and writing, and still have time to spend with my family."

Students in Katrina's introductory class meet with her six times during the fall semester and five times during the spring. She builds extensive one-on-one contact into her classes because she knows how valuable those conversations can be to aspiring lawyers and how rare they are in practice. "What I enjoyed most about working with summer associates and junior associates was meeting with them and talking with them about their writing. Now I get to do that every day," she says.

After teaching for a year in the Legal Writing and Analysis program, Katrina was asked to teach in the renowned Alternative Dispute Resolution program at Moritz as well. She taught a class on Legal Negotiations and Settlements, in which her students did a simulated negotiation in every class. "It was a lot of fun to teach," she says.

Katrina loves her work. "I feel like this job, at this school, is a gift. I get to help students with their writing and to give them the professional skills I found most valuable when I was practicing." She thought she would make a good professor, but she didn't know she would enjoy teaching as much as she does.

One of her work's most rewarding aspects is that it enables her to instill confidence in promising pre-lawyers. Her students, she notes, come to law school understandably nervous about their chances of finding a good job and whether they'll succeed and enjoy it when they do. "I can offer them hope," she says. "I met a lot of good, bright people in the legal profession, and I found a home there myself. I tell them that I see future lawyers when I look at them, even though they may not see it yet."

13

THE CONSULTANTS

One of my favorite ways to think about practicing lawyers is as trusted advisors. As a senior associate, reading *The Trusted Advisor* by David H. Maister, Charles H. Green, and Robert M. Galford changed my approach to work. If you find that advising clients is one of the most rewarding parts of practicing law, you might consider becoming a consultant instead. The ex-lawyers profiled in this section all serve as trusted advisors in various fields of expertise.

Greg Stone, a media consultant, changed his mind about practicing law while he was still in law school. He moved on to a career in journalism and video production. He encourages college students who are considering law school not to go unless they know with some specificity that they want to practice law. Being paid to worry about other people's problems, he notes, encourages a tendency to see problems everywhere instead of opportunities. His success has stemmed in part from recognizing opportunities when they came up instead of taking the more obvious path.

Greg Stone, Media Consultant

Greg Stone doesn't usually tell people he went to law school. As the owner of Stone Communications, the media consulting and production company he has run for more than twenty years, he finds the conversation more distracting than helpful. For Greg, law school was one turn in what became a long and successful media career. But it didn't look that way when he decided not to take a lucrative law firm job after getting his J.D.

Greg grew up in a close Italian family. His father was a lawyer, and the family expected Greg to follow suit. In his senior year at Harvard, his father passed away. Greg decided to go to Rutgers Law School, his father's alma mater.

"I hated law from day one," he says. Greg found it stultifying to be restricted by precedent. He cared about social policy, but saw no room for it in what he was studying. He liked writing but disliked the verbose writing style law school had instilled in him, a style it took him years to unlearn. At the time, he was still reeling from his father's death and he had no other adults to help guide him away from law and toward another career.

As he started his last year of law school, he got an offer to work for a firm at a salary so high that it terrified him. "I thought it was too much money at too young an age," he says. "I didn't want to get tied down." He had worked for other lawyers while he was still in school, and realized that he was going to hate that life.

With the law firm offer in hand, he considered other options. He had always wanted to be a reporter, so he typed 150 inquiry letters and sent them to newspapers all over the country. He also applied to Columbia Journalism School and got his acceptance before he received his J.D. When he got an offer from a New Haven paper as well, he had to decide what to do. Should he go straight into another graduate program or get some work experience?

He chose Columbia, thinking (correctly, as it turns out) that the name would open a lot of doors for him. He spent nine months working on a master's degree. His advisor praised his thesis, and his Columbia contacts helped him land a job at Time, Inc. as an apprentice writer.

The salary at Time, Inc. was roughly half of what he would have earned at the law firm, and money was tight. He slept on a friend's couch for a while, and then moved in with his girlfriend. "There were times when I questioned my decisions, but they were few and far between," he says. "I had faith in what I was doing."

After working on the in-house newsletter and freelancing for *Time* magazine, Greg went to work for *Money* as a fact-checker. When *Time* started an electronic magazine, Greg went to work there for three years. At the same time, he went back to graduate school, for the third time. *Time* had offered to send some of its best people to the part-time executive program at Columbia Business School. He worked from Monday to Thursday, then spent every Friday in class studying for his Master of Science in Business.

The Columbia program gave Greg an insight into a different lifestyle. "Everyone in that program was sponsored by their employer, so the school treated us like royalty. We had retreats at gorgeous conference centers. Although our Friday schedules were grueling, we got to have lunch at the Faculty Club."

His business degree from Columbia gave him the opportunity to continue living like royalty by going into investment banking, but he didn't like the investment bankers he met. "Life is too short to work with a bunch of jerks," he says. He may have missed more opportunities to make a fortune with his business degree than his law degree, but earning a big salary right away wasn't as important to him as the long-term conditions of his working life.

"I think you have to decide how much intangible things mean to you," he says. "Otherwise someone else's dollar figures could affect your decisions too much." Greg decided that having the freedom of being self-employed was worth $5 million to him. The goal of having his own media business drove almost every decision he made from then on. Greg set a goal for himself: to have his own business by the time he was thirty-five. "I was thirty-six when it happened," he says.

Just before he received his business degree, his division of *Time* folded and Greg got some severance. He left New York for an opportunity to work as a business reporter, first in

Minneapolis and then in Boston. Working with video teams in both cities, Greg became increasingly interested in "the power of the moving picture," as he puts it.

After three years in Boston, Greg was ready to start his own media production and consulting business. He set up Stone Communications in 1989 and has been his own boss ever since. He advises political candidates, senior executives, health-care providers, and nonprofits on all aspects of media. He also helps them prepare for interviews and produces videos for corporate clients.

Making a career change like Greg did isn't easy, even when you do it fairly early in your career. "You have to be really tough, especially when you have a credential that will push you in a certain direction," says Greg. "If you can swing it financially, you're better off doing what you want to do early on. I know so many lawyers who would rather be doing something else. They say they fell into it. And the older you get, the more your lifestyle is tied to your job and the harder it is to change."

Part of being tough, he notes, is taking the risks involved with an unfamiliar venture. But there are certain advantages to doing something unusual. If you are doing what you really want to do, he says, you'll develop the strength to explain it to people who don't understand your passion as well as you do. The rewards are tremendous. "You have to take a deep breath," he says, "and do what you love."

Greg's career trajectory took him fairly far from his beginnings in law school. He recognized early on that he didn't enjoy law, and moved into journalism instead. Working in journalism and then in video production allowed him to build a satisfying career consulting with clients on a subject he loves.

Moving from the wrong career to the right one doesn't always involve such a drastic change. Susannah Baruch, a policy consultant, has spent most of her career working on reproductive rights and genetic testing issues. She is passionate about these issues and has substantive expertise in them. Her career change was more a matter of form than substance. Instead of changing fields, she changed the way she works. While she began her career in lawmaking on Capitol Hill, she made a transition into consulting in order to harmonize her policy interests, her collaborative style, and her family priorities.

Susannah Baruch, Policy Consultant

Susannah Baruch grew up with a passion for social change, the only child of parents she describes as liberal and feminist. She was always interested in leadership and the battle of politics. After graduating from Yale, she worked for People for the American Way. She enjoyed her job, which involved watching televangelists and keeping track of their claims, and she liked the sense of being inside the Beltway fighting for truth and justice. During that year, the nation's attention focused on the Clarence Thomas hearings and a new awareness of sexual harassment emerged. Susannah's experience in D.C. confirmed that a J.D. was an important credential for anyone who wanted to be an advocate, as she did.

Susannah joined the minority of liberal students at University of Chicago Law School. She chose a school with a conservative reputation because she thought it would be the best place to hone her advocacy skills. The conservative environment also helped sharpen her identity as a public interest lawyer. Although law school reinforced her interest in advocacy, she found herself in the minority of students seeking careers in public interest law. She was one of the first University of Chicago students in many years to earn a Skadden Fellowship.

The fellowship funded two years of work at what was then the Women's Legal Defense Fund. She learned how to deal with Congress, which led to a job with Nita Lowey (D-NY). Her time in Representative Lowey's office allowed Susannah to work extensively on reproductive health issues in a context she found daunting at first.

"The Hill was, even more than law school, like jumping into a big ocean of hard," she says. It was hard to get things done, she says, because of the culture of "sharp elbows." The adversarial environment was especially frustrating because she found she could not be as effective in matters that were important to her as she wanted to be, primarily because she is not adversarial by nature.

After her time on the Hill, Susannah returned to what had become the National Partnership for Women and Families. She worked both on reproductive health issues and on the passage of the Genetic Information Non-Discrimination Act (GINA). She was also intrigued by a new think tank that was forming at Johns Hopkins. Its first focus would be reproductive genetics, the genetic testing before and during pregnancy, which Susannah found most interesting. Although the group was in its formative stages, Susannah knew the founder and "pestered her until she gave me a job," she says.

When she started working for the Genetics and Public Policy Center, Susannah had two small children. Several years later, when the funding for her permanent position evaporated, Susannah decided to become a consultant instead. Her children were seven and nine at the time, and, fortunately, her family could rely on her husband's work benefits. Consulting offered her a more flexible schedule and the opportunity to expand her contacts. Her first client was the Genetics and Public Policy Center. Her next client was Generations Ahead, a progressive ethics and social justice group based in Oakland, California.

Susannah eventually worked solely for Generations Ahead. She hadn't enjoyed soliciting other consulting clients. "The week I realized that I needed to figure out my future life as a consultant, I saw that the founder of Generations Ahead was advertising a full-time job. I had met this woman before and was impressed," she says. Susannah had been working four days a week since her children were born, and asked the founder to consider taking her on a four-day schedule. Generations Ahead agreed to her proposal.

In her first year, Susannah's work focused on the ethical and political issues around sex selection. Generations Ahead approached the issue differently from Susannah's previous employers because, as she puts it, "it was not a traditional D.C. organization." Rather than focusing on legislation, the group focused on increasing attention and generating a national conversation. Susannah continues to consult on this kind of policy work, and has a range of clients including the National Asian Pacific Women's Forum.

Susannah's work combines the same kind of research, analysis, and writing she has always liked with strategic planning designed to build consensus. For example, one of her projects involves websites offering blood tests to help determine fetal gender early in a pregnancy. A critical policy question is what an ideal website offering this service should look like, including what information it should disclose. One aspect of her research is designing a survey of people who have used the test, to determine what their experience was. Her team considers whether publishing their findings in a scientific journal or to a more general audience would draw more attention to the topic. Susannah's work analyzes all of these questions, with an eye toward developing a social policy that makes sense and, perhaps, informing future regulation of such websites.

In early 2013, Susannah's career took another turn when she agreed to serve as the interim president and CEO of the Reproductive Health Technologies Project. She took the role with the understanding on both sides that it was only a short-term position. Although she was invited to apply for the CEO position, she did not want to take a job that would require so much travel. She was also mindful that accommodating other people's schedules would limit her own potential for flexibility.

The short-term role appealed to Susannah because it allowed her to try on the kind of leadership position she may be more likely to take when her children are older. The experience surprised her. "I didn't expect that it would be so much fun," she says. "It's energizing to take on something big enough to be a real challenge."

At a macro level, Susannah's shift from Capitol Hill to consulting may not appear radical, but she has made important changes in what she does and how she works. "I was initially attracted to lobbying and arguing and getting bills passed, but now what interests me more is how you define the problem and craft a solution that has the support to move forward. This is important work, and I want to do it in a civil way. I see less civility at the higher levels." Instead of competing with the hard-nosed advocates who work to push laws through, she works on developing the intelligence necessary to define what those laws should look like to be most effective. Her work facilitates discussion instead of debate.

Susannah believes in the power of gradual transition. "You can't lay out the whole path in front of you," she says. "You put down one stepping-stone at a time and the path eventually appears, but it may not be the one you envisioned at first." The power of laying these stepping-stones, however, is significant. Susannah made her career choices in part because she felt strongly about maintaining a part-time schedule. "Our family has made choices about how we want our day-to-day lives to be," she says, "and it just wouldn't be possible with two full-time lawyer parents." When she looks at people with more highly paid, higher-status jobs, although she may have moments in which she wonders whether she made the right choice, overall she is relieved not to have to burn the candle at both ends.

Susannah's openness to new experiences, like serving as an interim CEO, illustrates an important tenet of successful career change. It helps to be open to experimentation. Any change that moves you out of your comfort zone is bound to be nerve-wracking at first. Those experiments, however, can reveal important truths about the right career for you.

Once the newness of the situation starts to wear off, you can start to evaluate whether you have gone in the right direction.

That, of course, is an intellectual as well as an intuitive decision. Susannah was surprised by how much fun it was to be in the CEO's seat. If and when she thinks about shifting from consulting to a more permanent role, that knowledge will help her make the right decision.

If, on the other hand, a new role or a new organization turns out to be the wrong step for you, you can always change your mind. Experimentation is valuable in helping you figure out what doesn't work, too. The key is having the courage to correct your path rather than continuing, for months or years, in the wrong direction.

Lisa Montanaro experimented with a new career as a professional organizer while she was still in law. That period of double tracking allowed Lisa to figure out whether she would be happy in her new field before she committed to it. It also allowed her to build the experience as a consultant and speaker that would help drive her success.

What I love about Lisa's story is that she does what she is. She found a way to turn the organizing, productivity, and performing skills that come naturally to her into a thriving business as a coach and consultant. As her interests have evolved from organizing to productivity to life coaching, so has her business.

Lisa Montanaro, Productivity Consultant

Lisa Montanaro draws on her skills as a performer, teacher, and lawyer in her current career as a productivity consultant and life coach. She launched a professional organizing business in 2002, after practicing law for seven years.

Lisa's first love was performing. Her comfort being onstage is clear when she teaches teleclasses on getting organized and gives motivational speeches. Before law school, she was a singer, actress, and dancer. She is also fluent in American Sign Language. She worked as an instructor and interpreter, which requires an element of performance, at the New York School for the Deaf while she went to law school at night.

Although she was passionate about the stage, she didn't come from a wealthy family. The idea of being a starving actress in New York wasn't appealing. While she was still in high school, she had started thinking about law as an alternative to acting. Law, she thought, would give her a chance to perform. The courtroom would be her stage. She intended to be a litigator, "which, in the end, was what I hated most," she says.

Lisa loved studying law. She had enrolled in the evening program at Pace Law School, and the evening students formed a close group. The practice of law was another matter entirely. She worked at a legal aid office during one summer, but in her third year she got an offer from Chadbourne & Parke. "I was wowed by the big firm," she says. "I had a lot of loans, and I told myself I couldn't save the world if I couldn't pay my rent." Lisa was the first person in her family to graduate from college, and she was proud to have an offer from such a prestigious firm. She was also flattered that anyone would pay her that much money. Lisa told herself that she would stay just until her loans were repaid.

As it happened, she was at the firm only eighteen months before her husband was accepted into veterinary school in Michigan and they moved. Lisa had been practicing employment law and litigation, and knew a lot about employment agreements. She taught a labor law course at Detroit College of Law as an adjunct. Although she loved teaching, and would return to it later in her career, she wasn't interested in the competitive world of legal academia. Her favorite law job was working as a staff attorney for the Michigan Education Association. She enjoyed her colleagues and not having a billable minimum. She also loved being part of a union, which provided generous benefits and compensatory time.

Her husband was then matched with a prestigious veterinary internship back in New York. While Lisa was excited to go back to New York, where she had spent most of her life, she wasn't as excited about the increased cost of living they would face on her income alone.

Lisa knew she didn't want to go back to a big firm. Although she had left Chadbourne on good terms, her experience there had been too scarring. As she started thinking about other options, she thought she might as well cast a wide net. One night, she was talking with her best friend about what else she might do. They started brainstorming about transferable skills. Her friend pointed out what a great organizer Lisa was. Lisa realized that it was true. At a small firm she worked for during her last year of law school, she had reorganized the firm's client files. She helped friends and family members organize their homes. It was something that came naturally to her, something she enjoyed.

When her friend said, "It's too bad you can't organize for a living," the light went on for both of them. "Actually, it was more like an explosion," Lisa says. Within an hour, she had found the website for the National Association of Professional Organizers (NAPO). She was stunned to learn that she could make a living from organizing other people's lives. Because Lisa needed to support both her husband and herself, it wasn't the right time to launch a new business. But it planted the seed for her next career.

Her Chadbourne connections, together with her employment law experience, led to her next job as in-house counsel at Pace University. She worked closely with the general counsel, who thought highly of her work and started grooming her as his replacement. Lisa respected her boss, but didn't want his job.

After her husband finished his internship and started earning more, Lisa looked into other careers that would allow her to use her law degree. "I wasn't miserable, but I knew I would leave law practice eventually," she says. She thought about law school career services and mediation, but nothing interested her more than the idea of becoming a professional organizer.

Rather than jumping in with both feet, Lisa started off slowly. She ran her organizing business at night and on weekends, while working in-house at Pace. She posted a quote above her computer at Pace that read: "Leap and the net shall appear."

She didn't feel comfortable leaping, however, until she had paid off her loans and saved some money. The threat of financial loss was her biggest fear. She built up a reserve in her bank account as a safety measure, so that she wouldn't go running back to the law if her new business didn't make money in its first year. "I was brave enough to leave, but cautious enough to plan," she says. "I was leaving law to be an organizer. It would be weird if I were not organized about it."

As Lisa got ready to leave Pace, she approached her boss with the news. To her surprise, he offered to let her work part time while she figured out whether the business was viable. "He gave me a huge gift," she says. Having her there part time also allowed Pace to do an executive search for her replacement. After her business launched, Pace became one of her biggest clients.

Her time at Chadbourne also paid off in her new business. Chadbourne lawyers and legal professionals attended some of the workshops Lisa created on organizing and time management for busy law professionals. Lisa developed such programs for the Bar of the Association of the City of New York, Pace Law School Continuing Education Programs, the National Association of Law Placement, and the New York City Legal Recruiters Association, among other groups.

Ten years after Lisa launched her business, she felt like she had earned an MBA without having to pay the tuition. She learned a lot about small business ownership by taking courses. At one point, she offered to run a program for New York–area entrepreneurs, for which she first had to learn everything in the curriculum. "I've always believed the student can become the master," she says.

Lisa is now an internationally recognized professional organizer, as well as a productivity consultant, life coach, and motivational speaker. She writes articles frequently, and her first book was published in 2011. While she knew she would love being an organizer, she says, she had no idea how much she would love being an entrepreneur. "I didn't know I would like owning a business until I found the right business for me."

14

THE ADVOCATES

Many people who go to law school hoping to make a difference in the world are sorely disappointed by the realities of law practice. The high cost of law school may make it impossible for lawyers with student loans to work for a legal services organization, at least right away, unless their schools offer a low income protection plan. Advocating for the corporate clients who can afford large law firms can be less than satisfying. Firms are increasingly reluctant to count pro bono work toward billable minimums, leaving fewer associates with the time and opportunity for public service.

While there is still a tremendous need for legal services, moving into public interest law later in your career can be difficult. Budget cuts at the state and federal level often mean cuts in the number of public interest law positions available. In filling those few positions, the best legal service providers look for a history of experience with and commitment to nonprofit work. Becoming a public interest lawyer after time in private practice often means taking a pay cut of 50 percent or more. The work can be enormously rewarding, but not usually in financial terms. Lawyers who are already in the field have to deal with increasing workloads, salary freezes, and often more troubling clients.

The ex-lawyers profiled in this section work as advocates outside the legal profession. They channel their passion and legal training to serve a group they care deeply about. Some of them remain close to the issues they focused on in private practice. Eleanor Hoague, for example, has been working with immigrants since she was in law school. She became a lawyer in part because she admired the work her father did on civil rights issues, and she inherited his passion for advocacy. Although she left law practice years ago, she still helps immigrants get access to justice. Counseling an immigrant community outside Seattle allows her to engage in a different form of service.

Eleanor Hoague, Immigrants' Rights Advocate

Eleanor Hoague has always thought of law and social justice as intertwined. Her father was the president of the Washington chapter of the American Civil Liberties Union. He practiced civil rights and immigration law as well. She and her sisters grew up admiring his work and the influence it had on the community. Eleanor, in particular, saw law as a way to do good in the world.

Her decision to go to law school was grounded in that idealism. At the time, she says, "a lot of people I knew were going into law because we wanted to make the world a better place." She worked with immigrants in local prisons while she was still in law school. She spoke fluent Spanish, and loved helping her immigrant clients.

When she graduated from law school, around the time of the Cuban boat lift, she started her own firm with a partner. Many of the people Fidel Castro sent into exile had been in jail and/or mental institutions in Cuba, and the ones who admitted as much at the United States border were detained. Hundreds of these detainees were transferred to the McNeil Island Penitentiary near Tacoma, Washington, close to Eleanor's new firm.

Eleanor led a group of lawyers and translators representing these immigrants, in part because of the counseling experience she had had in law school. She had only been out of school for a year, but her group's work made headlines when it resisted the government's efforts to transfer the immigrants en masse.

When that crisis was over, Eleanor accepted an offer to go in-house with a corporation that did work in Latin America. Although she had spent time in Mexico, Eleanor didn't expect the company to be as male-dominated as it was. She stuck it out for almost four years, until the supervisor she liked moved to another company. She looked for a graceful way to leave.

Instead of quitting outright, she worked on a postdoctoral degree at Cambridge University and applied for a Fulbright scholarship in Argentina. When she won the Fulbright, she moved to Argentina. She thought about practicing law there, but there was no need for her expertise. American lawyers were used mostly to help set up corporations in the U.S., which she wasn't interested in doing.

While she was in Argentina, she taught English at a prestigious school. She was also invited to work on one of the first English/Spanish legal dictionaries, which she thoroughly enjoyed. At the same time, she began to realize that she would always be seen as "la Americana," and she didn't want to be an expatriate forever. She moved back to Seattle in 1989 and reconnected with a man she had met before she left, whom she later married.

Eleanor thought her experience would be valuable in Seattle, but found no success with the local firms. She started another practice, handling divorce cases for lower-income clients. "I hated that," she says. "It was hard to separate my clients' experiences from my own." In addition to the emotional drain, she wasn't making much money. This went on for years.

Eleanor felt stuck. She'd gone into law intending to help the public, but she didn't feel like she was helping anyone other than a few of her clients. Her clients, on the whole, were often hard to deal with because they were in crisis so much of the time. When they called her in the middle of the night to talk about their problems, Eleanor found it hard to shut them out.

She also grew concerned about the effect her work was having on her. Many of the attorneys on the other side of her cases were hostile, often to the brink of bullying. Eleanor, to her surprise, became aggressive in response. She found that she could be more effective in getting concessions by being unpleasant. "Law brought out a side of me that I didn't like," she says. In addition, she started to doubt that practicing law was the best use of her talents. She had met some brilliant lawyers, and she didn't feel like she was as talented as they were.

When her father passed away, she inherited enough money to stop working for a while. Soon afterward, the bilingual dictionary she had cowritten in Argentina was finally published, and she started receiving royalty checks. When her newly widowed mother accidentally hit her head and needed constant care, Eleanor was able to provide it.

She started thinking about what else she could do. She enrolled in a course called Running from the Law, taught by Deborah Arron, which was affiliated with a book of the same name. The course cracked open the possibility that she didn't have to be an attorney forever. "The reality of practicing law is abysmal," she says. The lack of honor in the profession disappoints her too. "It used to be a relatively small world, and you could rely on other lawyers keeping their word. People are less trustworthy than they used to be."

After her mother passed away, Eleanor returned to work, but not as a lawyer. She coauthored a second edition of the English–Spanish legal dictionary, which had been more successful than she expected.

When that project ended, she started advising immigrants with legal problems and organizations such as the Northwest Immigration Legal Services. That experience helped her see that she could work with the immigrant population without actually practicing law.

Eleanor now lives on an island near Seattle that has a large immigrant population. Her main role is advising illegal immigrants about how strong their case is likely to be and whether they should get a lawyer. She has a good reputation in that community as someone who tells it straight and knows the system. She also knows the dangers of bad representation. She tries to warn people away from lawyers who, for example, go on vacation when a hearing is scheduled without giving their clients notice of the hearing, which usually results in the client's deportation. Rather than representing the clients directly, she refers them to one of several law firms whose work she respects.

Eleanor appreciates how hard it is to walk away from a legal career. For her, making a break allowed her the space to rediscover what she had loved in the first place: helping immigrants get the assistance they need, without acting as a lawyer herself. Although she knows it can be hard to rediscover something that motivates you, she points out that the alternative is worse. "You can either go on being miserable or you can stretch your head around doing something different," she says.

While some advocates stay close to the issues they had worked on as lawyers, like Eleanor Hoague, others decide to turn their volunteer work into a full-time advocacy role. Deborah Felton had been out of the legal world for eighteen years before she became the executive director of Fuller Village, a senior residence south of Boston. She had served on its board of directors for several years, and knew the community well. During that time, the other board members had come to appreciate her advocacy and leadership skills. Deborah had developed a strong reputation as someone who could get things done and work effectively with a broad range of people. When the executive director position opened up, Deborah was a natural fit. One of the most rewarding aspects of her job is the opportunity to serve as an advocate for both Fuller Village itself and all of its residents.

Deborah Felton, Executive Director of Senior Residence

Deborah Felton is a born leader. Before she went to law school, she worked as a paralegal for some lawyers she admired, including some women. "I thought I should go to law school and be in charge," she says. She believed strongly in the importance of advocating for other people. At the age of twenty-seven, she started law school and set her sights on a public interest career.

Deborah worked at the Department of Justice before moving to the Federal Election Commission for a year. She then spent two years at the state's Ethics Commission. After she had her first child, Deborah opened her own practice handling child abuse cases. She had another daughter two years later.

As her daughters grew, having a flexible schedule became more important to Deborah. Her children are biracial, and grew up in a predominantly white community. There were times when it was especially important for Deborah to advocate for them.

The court system she worked with, however, wasn't so flexible. Deborah often found herself before a judge who would not call her cases until the late afternoon. At the time, her husband was prosecuting domestic violence cases and didn't have much flexibility in his schedule either.

Deborah decided to take time off when she became pregnant with her third daughter. She transferred the energy she had poured into her legal work to community programs instead. She became an advocate in her town, and quickly developed a reputation for effectiveness. People would go to her when they needed help with a local issue. "I realized you can effect change as long as people realize that you're an ally, not an enemy," she says.

Deborah was invited to join the board of directors of Fuller Village, a senior residence in town. The executive director knew that Deborah was smart, committed, and dependable. Soon after Deborah joined the board, the president of the board was in a car accident. Deborah was asked to take on more of a leadership role. She ran the board of directors meetings while he recuperated.

After she had been on the board for four years, the executive director position came open. Her fellow board members wanted Deborah to take it, and she considered it seriously. At that point, she had been out of the paid workforce for eighteen years. She was ready to go back.

Returning to the legal profession, however, seemed too daunting. She knew it would take her a lot of time and effort to catch up on the legal and technological developments she had missed in the interim. More importantly, she wanted to run her own show. She had honed her leadership skills in the community for years. She was a great leader, and she didn't want to apply those skills as a bureaucrat in an organization that she didn't really care about.

She did care about Fuller Village, and she knew it well. Becoming the executive director would allow her to use her skills in negotiation, advocacy, and organizational management. It would allow her to speak publicly about care of the elderly, a cause that is growing in importance.

Getting the position wasn't as difficult as it would have been if she were a stranger to the organization. She had the full support of her board, who knew she would be a good fit, so she didn't have to go through a battery of draining interviews. She was fifty-five when she took on the executive director role.

It suits her perfectly. "If I had ever taken a professional aptitude test, this probably would have come up as my ideal job," she says. She enjoys thinking on her feet, considering all sides, and then making decisions, and in the process using leadership skills that she learned in law school.

She also enjoys having the opportunity to interact with a variety of people every day. Fuller Village has forty-five staff members, some of whom are part time, and four hundred residents. She likes mentoring her staff, because it allows her to use her good judgment and experience for their benefit. She also appreciates having a flexible schedule, which, as the boss, she can give herself.

Most importantly, Deborah enjoys advocating for the residents. She has been an advocate all her life, whether she was acting on behalf of her legal clients, her daughters, or her community. "It is who I am," she says. She enjoys using her persuasive skills to help the residents get the help they need, and to work in partnership with their families when necessary.

Deborah loves her work, but she's not planning to do it forever. "I'll do this for another few years and then think about finding a beach somewhere," she says.

Jen Atkins' transition from law to nursing is one of the more radical changes described in this book, but it makes perfect sense in light of Jen's overall goals and priorities. In law school, she had enjoyed helping consumers get out of credit card debt. For most of her legal career, however, she didn't have the opportunity to help people in a similarly gratifying way. She wanted to find work that would allow her to be an advocate again, permit a flexible schedule, and give her the chance to make a broader impact on society. Becoming a nurse checked all of those boxes.

It wasn't easy for Jen to go to nursing school in her thirties, with three kids at home. The courage and stamina she showed in doing so led to her current role as a cardiac nurse in one of the best children's hospitals in the country. Jen hopes to draw on both her nursing experience and her legal training to advocate on health-care policy issues later in her career.

Although some people are puzzled by her change of career, Jen loves being an advocate for her patients. As she explains, "I like taking care of people, and feel a lot better about doing it as a nurse than as a lawyer."

Jen Atkins, Nurse

Jen Atkins doesn't usually tell people she was a lawyer before she became a nurse. "I generally just tell people this is my second career," she says.

Jen grew up in a political family. As a kid, she stood with her parents outside polling places holding a handmade sign. After getting her degree in political science from Boston University, she moved to Washington for an internship in Congress. She applied to law school intending to work for a group like the National Organization for Women after graduation. When she looked at the size of her loans, however, she decided to go in a different direction so that she could pay them off as soon as possible.

While she was in law school, she became interested in consumer bankruptcy. She was troubled by the number of credit card companies deluging unqualified people with card offers and by the number of consumers filing for bankruptcy. She enjoyed the work she did during law school for the leaders of the National Association of Consumer Bankruptcy Attorneys.

Jen's experience with bankruptcy led her to interview with accounting firms instead of law firms. She joined Deloitte's tax advising practice, and then moved to Pricewaterhouse-Coopers. She liked being part of a prestigious corporate brand, with perks that included training sessions held at fancy resorts twice a year.

At the same time, her job was intensely demanding. She worked the same hours she would have at a law firm, but at a lower salary. A larger problem was that she didn't believe in the mission. Ultimately, her goal was to help clients pay less in taxes. State governments needed that tax income, she thought, to pay teachers and fix potholes. "I didn't feel good about my job and I was looking to leave, even though I was doing well," she says.

While she was considering her options, Jen became pregnant with her first child. She intended to go back to work when her maternity leave ended, but realized that she didn't like her job enough to put her daughter in day care for it.

At that point, she wasn't sure what to do. She did not necessarily want to stay home full time. Going back wasn't appealing. She considered the part-time option PwC offered, a four-day week in exchange for a 20 percent pay cut, but knew there was no guarantee that she would actually end up working fewer hours than on a full-time schedule.

It took some time for Jen to decide on her next step. She had two more children. As much as she loved being with her kids, she wanted another focal point. She lost touch with her work friends, and felt isolated at home.

When she thought about what parts of her working life had brought her the most satisfaction, she didn't think of accounting. Instead, she thought of how rewarding it had been to help clients facing bankruptcy who were being harassed by creditors. While she was home, she kept asking the same question: What could she do that would let her advocate for vulnerable people again?

She thought about how much she admired the nurses who had helped her in the hospital with her children. She knew that she didn't want to go to medical school, but she was intrigued by the idea of nursing.

At the same time, part of her fought the idea. She had invested so much time and money in law school that it would be foolish, she thought, to change direction. In order to become a nurse, she would need either a second bachelor's degree or an associate's degree. The associate's degree programs were less expensive, but the bachelor's degree was more marketable. There were prerequisite classes for the bachelor's degree in anatomy, chemistry, and microbiology, none of which she had taken.

Jen thought that it would be impossible for her to do any of this. At the time, she had three kids under the age of five "and two elderly dogs," she points out. She didn't tell anyone that she was thinking about nursing. When she finally told her husband that she might want to go back to school and become a nurse, he said he thought she should do it. She was surprised. His support helped Jen give herself permission to pursue the idea of nursing. If she was going to do this, she thought, she might as well go for the program that would give her the best job prospects.

She started taking night classes in the prerequisite courses at a local community college during the summer of 2008. After she started her coursework, her husband was laid off from his job, and their family was profiled in a national magazine article about the effects of the recession. She thought briefly about trying to get her job in tax consulting back, but realized that that would be nearly impossible in the economy as it was then.

Two years after she started night classes, as her fortieth birthday approached, she entered the highly regarded nursing program at Simmons College. "Nursing school was so much harder than law school," she says. "Maybe that's because I was in my forties instead of my twenties." She was initially reluctant to tell her classmates that she was a lawyer, since others weren't always kind about it, but the truth came out in the course of class bonding. She graduated from Simmons in May 2012.

Jen is now a staff nurse in inpatient cardiology at Boston Children's Hospital, one of the top children's hospitals in the country. Her patients range from infants to adults who are being followed by their pediatric doctors, all of whom have congenital or acquired heart conditions or defects.

The excitement Jen feels about her new career is palpable. She sees nursing as an advocacy profession. What she loves most about nursing, she says, is the opportunity to look out for her patients when they are most vulnerable. "The nurse is the patient's first and last protection," she explains. "We make sure they understand what their doctors are telling them, and we make sure that they're receiving what they are supposed to receive." Mistakes get made, she says, and nurses are in the best position to look out for those mistakes. She also values the flexibility nursing offers, especially as she contemplates the changes in her kids' needs as they get older.

Jen's long-term goal is to get involved in health-care policy. "I'm still a political person," she says, "and I see health care as one of the most important policy grounds our country will face in the future." Knowing that she will use her nursing experience in tandem with her legal skills to further a social goal she cares so much about comforts her. "I have finally done what I wanted to do from the beginning and I had some great experiences in the middle," she says.

Making a radical change may appear to require superhuman confidence, but Jen says that's not the case. She developed her courage step by step along the way. "The more pressure you take on, the more you find you can bear," she says. "It's like mothers who hold their children in their arms every day. They start when the children are babies. As they grow, the mothers become stronger without seeming to notice the effort."

15

THE HEALERS

Some ex-lawyers find that working in a healing profession allows them to help people more directly or in more rewarding ways than they could as lawyers. All of the ex-lawyers profiled here benefited from someone else in the profession they later entered themselves. Clare Dalton, the renowned law professor and advocate for domestic violence victims, found relief from her own pain in acupuncture. That experience led her to leave academia and become an acupuncturist herself. Van Lanckton had been studying with rabbis for years before deciding to go to rabbinical school himself, at an age when many of his colleagues were starting to retire. Will Meyerhofer's own experiences in therapy helped him see that being a therapist would be a more rewarding use of his skills than being an associate at a big Manhattan firm.

Liz Mirabile also discovered her post-law career as a health coach after suffering health problems of her own. When her doctors could neither diagnose nor treat her allergies effectively, she found relief in a specialized allergy technique. She now treats other people using the same technique along with other therapies. Liz uses the analytical skills she learned in law school to help her clients sort through conflicting health advice. The counseling skills that she once used as an estate planning lawyer are now used to help her clients improve their health.

Becoming a health coach allowed Liz to work in a field she had become passionate about. It also lets her work with clients in a way that is compatible with her values, on a schedule compatible with her family's needs.

Liz Mirabile, Health Coach

Liz Mirabile practiced law at one of Boston's largest and most prestigious law firms for several years. She is now a health coach who specializes in helping people who have chemical, environmental, and food allergies. She can empathize with her clients because of her own experiences suffering from sudden, severe allergic reactions in her late thirties.

As an undergraduate, Liz studied psychology, hoping to do something that would help others. Working as a teaching assistant and volunteering at two local mental hospitals helped her realize that she didn't want to become a psychologist. She volunteered for a year at the National Organization for Women and Planned Parenthood before deciding to apply to law school.

During her first summer, she worked in the domestic violence unit at the Middlesex County District Attorney's office. She found it harder, scarier, and more emotionally draining to advocate for victims than she expected. One serial abuser made it clear to her that he had found her name and knew where she went to law school.

After graduation, Liz joined the trusts and estates group at a large Boston firm. Trusts and estates work, she reasoned, would give her the opportunity to counsel clients. She enjoyed solving complex problems for clients, but only occasionally got the chance to meet them in person. She soon realized that she didn't have the drive to stay there. "I knew I wasn't going to make partner because I didn't want it badly enough," she says.

"I didn't want to sacrifice my life." Even the senior partner in her department was in his office at midnight, and Liz didn't want that kind of life for herself. Like many women, it was also hard for her to find mentors in her firm. The women in her department were pushed so far beyond their limits that they had little time for mentoring others.

At the same time, Liz wasn't helping her clients in the way she had envisioned. "I love cracking the problem of how best to help people, and the complex and intricate planning that comes from high-end trusts and estates work," she says, "but I didn't find enough passion in that kind of work. It was intellectually engaging, but not emotionally satisfying. Helping someone figure out how to pay less in taxes didn't make my heart sing, even if that person might endow a library with the savings."

Considering her alternatives in the legal field, she started to look at smaller firms. "I was somewhat horrified to learn that everyone in those firms was working just as hard and was just as stressed out as lawyers at the larger firms, but they were earning a lot less for their sacrifices," she says. She thought about doing contract work, but couldn't find someone who was willing to do the business-generation piece that she didn't think she was experienced enough to do. "I got to the point where, for every door I went up to, there was a good reason to not go through it."

Liz left her firm after her first child was born. When her second child started kindergarten, she started thinking harder about going back to work. "I had this nightmare of being a hovering mother who is entirely involved with my kids," she says.

After being home with her children for several years, however, her health started to go downhill. In a single traumatic year, one of her parents passed away and the other nearly died. Liz lost an alarming amount of weight, and developed sensitivities to the environment so severe that she found it difficult to go out in public. "If I walked by the candle store at the mall, I couldn't breathe," she recalls. "I would get sick if someone was wearing perfume on an elevator. I thought I might become agoraphobic because it was so hard to go anywhere." None of the doctors she consulted could figure out what was wrong or how to treat her.

Liz started seeing a local healer named Amy Thieringer who had developed a procedure named Allergy Release Technique (ART). The ART process combines acupressure and homeopathy with techniques to manage the anxiety often associated with severe allergies. The treatments worked startlingly well. As Liz recovered, she decided to learn more about the process, first working with Amy to help manage her wait list and develop training materials.

Liz got a degree as a health coach from the Institute for Integrative Nutrition, a process that took more than a year, and then trained with Amy in ART. With her new degree and growing expertise, she opened her own practice.

As she gained proficiency in the allergy work, she decided to learn Reiki, a form of energy healing, and incorporate it into her work. Reiki can be an effective stress reliever. "Stress plays a role in many of my patients' allergies," she explains. It is stressful to be sick and unable to find a cause or solution, and the physical and emotional effects of stress can aggravate underlying conditions. "A lot of the clients I see are accomplished, articulate professionals, but talking about their stress doesn't relieve them of it."

Liz also advises her clients about nutrition, and explains the connection between diet and allergies. The holistic approach to treatment has a powerful impact on her clients. Liz's practice is growing from client referrals alone.

In her transition, Liz discovered an entrepreneurial side to herself that she hadn't known about. "I wanted to be the master of my destiny," she says.

Her newly flexible schedule also gives her more peace of mind. When she first considered going back to work, she had thought about starting a solo law practice, but didn't want to subject herself to the kind of time-sensitive crises that she would have been solely responsible for handling. "It had a level of intrusiveness that I couldn't tolerate," she explains.

As a health coach, however, Liz sets her own hours. She can schedule her clients around the needs of her family, rather than vice versa. If one of her clients has an urgent problem, Liz will see him, but those issues can generally be resolved in an hour or so. They don't hijack an entire weekend, or a family birthday celebration, the way a legal problem would.

Liz is grateful to have been able to step back from her first career and decide what she really wanted her life to look like. It's an experience she highly recommends. "If you find something you're passionate about and put all of yourself into it, you'll succeed. I don't know any case where it hasn't worked," she says. "And it is so, so worth the effort. I feel like I was living half a life as a lawyer. You may give up the prestige and the money, but you find yourself in the process. You'll find the life you want."

Clare Dalton has been one of my role models for more than twenty years, for both her brilliance and her bravery. In 1987, she sued Harvard Law School for sex discrimination when she was denied tenure. She won her case, but she didn't go back to Harvard—which was my loss, because I didn't get to study with her when I arrived a few years later. Instead, she went to Northeastern and used some of her settlement from Harvard to help create a domestic violence institute to advocate for victims. In short, she was a model of the lawyer many lawyers want to be: someone who used her brilliant legal mind to teach students, advocate for the underserved, and go up against the system when she was treated unfairly herself. And she didn't have to bill her hours.

When Clare left academia to open her own acupuncture practice, many people questioned her transition. In my view, her career change makes perfect sense. She has dedicated her life to helping other people in one form after another. She now heals clients by using her hands rather than helping students and victims of domestic violence by using her brain. She also has a history of choosing the more difficult option when she knew it was right for her, and ultimately benefiting society as a whole. How many lawyers can say that?

Clare Dalton, Acupuncturist

As one of the country's most distinguished legal scholars, Clare Dalton's academic career spanned more than thirty-five years. When Clare decided to become an acupuncturist, she did so out of love for a practice that had changed her own life. That practice led her organically and surprisingly in a different direction.

Lawyers who aren't familiar with Clare's scholarship or academic leadership may know her for another reason. In 1987, she made national headlines when she sued Harvard Law School for sex discrimination in denying her tenure and won her case. When she joined the faculty of Harvard Law School, she was already an accomplished lawyer and scholar.

As a student at Oxford, Clare's first love was literature and acting. Her father had been an English professor, as had his father. He raised her to believe that she could do anything she wanted, but encouraged her to study law instead of literature. "He thought we'd had too many generations of English teachers in the family already," she says. After getting her law degree, she accepted a position teaching legal writing at the University of Connecticut, and then got her LLM degree from Harvard Law School.

At Harvard, she started reading about feminism and the law. Her studies woke her up to the sexism she hadn't appreciated as such while she was at Oxford. When she joined Covington & Burling's Washington office a year later, she saw the disparity between men and women's experience of law practice. Clare practiced at Covington for almost four years before joining the Harvard Law School faculty in 1981.

When Harvard denied her tenure petition in 1987, she knew there could be no intellectual basis for the school's decision. She could not tolerate the attack on her intellectual integrity without fighting back. In the end, she won her case. "You come through those grueling experiences a stronger person," she says.

Rather than going back to Harvard, Clare joined the faculty of Northeastern Law School in 1988. When she came to Northeastern, some admiring students asked her to help them start a clinical program on domestic violence. She agreed, on the condition that the students help her learn about the issue. As she studied the sociological aspects of domestic violence, she realized that her own family had probably been affected by it. Reading about the generational transfer of its psychological impacts, she recognized a pattern of behavior she had seen firsthand. "I was looking at a form of sexism and hierarchy that I hadn't paid much attention to before," she says.

Running a domestic violence clinic was a new world, integrating law and psychology. "To do good legal work on domestic violence issues, you have to understand the psychological dynamics of it," she explains. Her clinic worked with community partners in order to maximize its impact. Writing grant applications for the new clinic also led to her first experience of rejection. When she learned more about the specifics of grant writing, her efforts were more successful.

Although Clare worked in academia from 1974 to 2010, her roles varied over the course of her career. She spent part of her career in traditional teaching and scholarship. She trained students to represent domestic violence victims in court. Later, she was a grant writer and administrator, supervising postgraduate fellows and chairing community boards. Clare was also Northeastern's assistant dean for academic affairs for two years. After winning an award for distinguished teaching in 2000, she completed a domestic violence casebook.

"All of these jobs were ways to explore whether I liked stretching myself in different directions," she says. The diverse experiences allowed her to figure out what she liked (teaching, mentoring) and didn't like (grant writing, fundraising). Over time, she came to favor the collegiality of the domestic violence institute over the solitude of traditional academia.

Then, something shifted at home. In the early 2000s, her marriage began to show signs of wear. Her two sons were out of the house, and her husband, Robert Reich, had lost his bid to become the next governor of Massachusetts. "There are times when one important piece in your life falls out, and it puts everything else into question," she says. "Or, you could say, it opens up a new set of opportunities." Clare later separated from her husband.

Clare's health began to suffer. She developed back pain and had bouts of diverticulitis. When she had taken all the medicine her doctors could give her, she looked into other practices, including yoga, Pilates, and meditation. On a friend's recommendation, she also started seeing an acupuncturist in Cambridge. The results were amazing. After her third appointment, she realized she had been hiding some emotional knowledge from herself. She was fascinated. "I wanted to know how a medicinal practice that puts needles into people could have an emotional effect on them as well," she says.

She decided to take an upcoming sabbatical in Oxford, where she had studied as an undergraduate. She saw it as an opportunity to experiment with living comfortably with less. It was also a chance to go back to the place her legal career began and think about the path not taken. When she thought about the parts of her career that had been the most rewarding, she thought about helping victims of domestic violence find relief. What she had liked most, she saw, was being of service.

Clare continued her acupuncture treatments in Oxford, and learned that there was an acupuncture school nearby. The school was one of few in the world that taught Five Element Acupuncture, the style of acupuncture she most admired. She asked whether she might just audit a course. The school said no. Denied the "light" option, Clare enrolled in the school for the first year of acupuncture training.

After her sabbatical ended and she returned to Boston, she went back to Oxford for three-day intensives every few months. She then had to make a decision. It wouldn't be easy to get the degree that would allow her to practice acupuncture herself. The nearest Five Element school was in Gainesville, Florida. The Gainesville school told her that she could transfer into their program if she passed the first year exams, which she did.

She took a leave of absence from Northeastern and moved to Florida for her final year of study. In that year, she learned to place needles in patients herself. Her final exams covered the foundations of Chinese medicine, acupuncture point location, and biomedicine. Clare prepared in part by taking community college courses in Florida and by taking courses online while working part time at Northeastern.

On campus, Clare didn't talk much about her new studies at first. "I was a little embarrassed," she says. "I worried that it might color my whole career, and that some people might think I was a dilettante." She expected that some of her colleagues would be skeptical. What she didn't anticipate was that for every skeptic, another person would come into her office, close the door, and tell her how wonderful they thought this new direction was.

The number of supporters caused her to ask herself whether she was censoring her own enthusiasm. "I decided to just lighten up," she says. "If I was immersed enough in what I was learning, and convinced of its value, then it was nothing to be ashamed of." She left Northeastern in 2010, after more than twenty years at the school, to start her own acupuncture practice.

In starting a second career at close to sixty, Clare neither wanted nor needed a full-time job. She was starting to have grandchildren. She wanted to spend some time near the oceans and countryside. She wanted time to cook. Clare acknowledges that she is lucky to have had the financial buffer to make her change, since she had been building up her retirement fund for many years. Clare decided to set up a part-time practice, seeing clients in Boston and Cambridge a few days a week. She reserves the rest of her time for the rest of her life.

When Clare left Northeastern, she had only a few clients. *The Boston Globe* then ran a story on her career transition, bringing her an influx of clients. She had fifty phone calls after the article first appeared, and she has been as busy as she wants to be ever since.

Clare's age and experience are assets to her practice. "My gray hair brings a lot of older people to me," she says. "People come to me for acupuncture because they know I come from a linear, rational tradition that is closer to their own lives. They think that if I take it seriously, maybe it is worth a shot." That said, Clare does not flaunt her career in legal academia. Her acupuncture website notes only that this is her second career.

Clare believes that the effort of trying to conform to a mold that doesn't suit you is, at the least, dangerous to your health and can in some cases be deadly. She has clients and former colleagues who still struggle to meet expectations, without fully appreciating the physical toll it is taking on them. "If you feel stuck, it can be easier to tell yourself that you can still make it work than to work instead toward a change," she says. "But when your lifestyle isn't congruent with who you are, it shows up in your body." She considers it a privilege to help heal her clients' bodies, as she inspires other lawyers to heal their lives.

Clare's transition from academia to acupuncture surprised many former colleagues and students. Similarly, Van Lanckton's transition from lawyer to rabbi surprised many of his former colleagues and clients. In fact, it's hard to pick the most surprising thing about Van Lanckton's career change. It could be that he started his six years of rabbinical school at age sixty. It could be that he wasn't born Jewish, and did not convert to Judaism until he was in his twenties. It could be that he is one of several lawyers-turned-rabbis in the Boston area alone.

Van himself had been thinking about becoming a rabbi for

some time. When a new rabbinical school opened up near his home, he knew it was time to make the change. His story, like so many others in this book, illustrates the importance of self-knowledge and a willingness to take risks when the opportunity presents itself.

Van Lanckton, Rabbi

Van Lanckton loves being a rabbi. He retired from the firm where he had spent the last twenty years of his legal career in order to enroll in full-time study in rabbinical school. When he started rabbinical school in 2003, he was sixty years old. He graduated six years later.

Making the transition from lawyer to rabbi is only one of his major life changes. He converted to Judaism in his twenties, completing the process a few months before he graduated from Harvard Law School in 1967. Growing up in Darien, Connecticut, which famously had a "Gentlemen's Agreement" among real estate agents not to sell to Jews, Van used to think Jews were just a historical concept. "I learned about the Jews in Jesus's time in Sunday School, but I never met any, so I assumed they weren't around anymore," he says.

After law school, Van taught in the legal services clinic Harvard had recently opened in Cambridge. He soon became its director and a teaching fellow in law and clinical practice at Harvard Law School. When Massachusetts created a cabinet system of government in 1971, he worked first for the Executive Office of Human Services, and then as general counsel for what was then called the Department of Public Welfare.

His next change came when his older son turned twelve. "Then I entered into the valley of the shadow of college," he says. After twelve years on the public side of law, Van joined the large Boston firm then known as Bingham, Dana & Gould. After three years, he moved to a smaller firm, where he practiced law for the next twenty years.

Another turning point came as he recovered from triple bypass surgery in 2001. He had been having chest pains for a while, but had tried to keep them from his wife and colleagues because he didn't want to take time off from work. Eventually, a perceptive doctor put him in the hospital for an immediate operation, which saved his life. As he recovered, he thought a lot about a single question: For what purpose had his life been saved? Van started thinking more deeply about what he wanted to do next.

The idea of becoming a rabbi came to him quickly. Nothing else seemed viable. "It was either lawyer or rabbi," he says. At that time, however, the closest rabbinical school was in New York. Enrolling there would mean either being away from his family during the week or moving his family to New York, neither of which appealed to him. As he was considering his options, he learned that Hebrew College was about to open a rabbinical school one mile from his house. He decided immediately to apply. "If they hadn't opened the school, I might still be a lawyer," he says.

Van joined the first class of rabbinical students, and graduated when he was sixty-six. One of the greatest surprises about rabbinical school, he says, was his classmates. "It hadn't occurred to me how lovely it would be to study with the kind of people who want to be rabbis," he says. "They are genuinely kind, caring, openhearted, and emotionally available people. I'll just say that there had been very little hugging going on at my law firm. I had no idea how much joy there would be in finding that community."

In retrospect, the transition from lawyer to rabbi was almost natural for him. He had been studying Talmud with a group in downtown Boston for many years, and had been giving sermons at the largest synagogue in New England, where he was an active member, for years before he went to rabbinical school. He had been a leader in the Jewish community, serving as president of the American Jewish Congress of New England

and chair of its Committee on Law and Social Action. His son became a rabbi thirteen years before he did, and is now the Jewish chaplain at a leading Boston hospital.

As Van points out, there are many similarities between lawyers and rabbis. Being a rabbi is "simply studying law from a higher authority," he notes. "And sermons are just like closing arguments, with no judge or opposing counsel." The counseling aspect is different, however. "When you counsel clients as a lawyer, they have a fixed set of options. When you're counseling congregants, you are mostly just listening."

For Van, changing careers was "a million-dollar decision," as he puts it. When he compares what he would have earned as a lawyer in the years since he resigned to what he has earned as a rabbi, he thinks the differential is about a million dollars. But it's not money he needed, he points out.

Van finds being a rabbi enormously satisfying. "The opportunity to accompany people both at times of great joy and great sadness is an amazing gift," he says. "Whether you help name a child, help that child pass through the rites of puberty as a bar mitzvah, marry people, or be with them when they are sick or dying, these are chances to assist people that you just don't get as a lawyer, even when you represent individuals." When he practiced law, there was a limit to the amount of stress his clients were under because their problems were financial. In contrast, he says, the help he can give as a rabbi is priceless.

Van also loves the intellectual stimulation of studying ancient texts and drawing lessons from them for life in modern times. He enjoys having colleagues who share his views about what a privilege it is to be a rabbi. He is also helping to shape his own community. Van used his legal training to create an alumni association for fellow graduates of Hebrew College's seminary, which is nondenominational and whose graduates serve different kinds of congregations.

Van believes strongly in living the examined life. As a rabbi, he often talks with people who are unhappy with their careers.

He recalls counseling one person in his fifties who wanted to be a social worker, but who hesitated to make the transition because he would be fifty-five by the time he finished his qualifications. Van pointed out that he would be fifty-five eventually anyway, and asked his congregant to think deeply about how he wanted to spend those years. "You get only one life," he says, "and you should do what you love, if you can find it."

Will Meyerhofer gives the same advice to his clients. His story illustrates what can happen when you have the courage to start again, and in his case, to start again twice. Will went from being miserable as an associate to being happier in marketing to loving his current work as a psychotherapist. After some hard start-up years, he now has as many clients as he wants. He likes being his own boss and setting his own schedule. He finds it immensely rewarding to help people live better lives on a daily basis.

Will knows, from personal experience and that of his clients, the value of figuring out what is truly going to make you happy. "If you miss that challenge," he says, "you miss a real opportunity for joy."

Will Meyerhofer, Psychotherapist

Will Meyerhofer, a New York psychotherapist in private practice, resisted going into the mental health field for a long time. Psychotherapy is his third and most satisfying career. His online forum, *The People's Therapist*, is especially popular among lawyers. Will knows from personal experience what their work lives are like.

As an undergraduate at Harvard, he spent a lot of time counseling people. Among his friends, and then their friends, he developed a reputation as a good listener who kept secrets. There was no shortage of Harvard undergrads who needed someone trustworthy to talk to. "I was everyone's therapist," he says.

In fact, Will came from a family of therapists. His father is a psychiatrist and his mother and brother are psychotherapists. His brother suggested that Will might enjoy being a therapist too, but Will headed to New York University School of Law instead. After graduation, he joined the New York office of Sullivan & Cromwell.

Will hated the adversarial nature of law firm work from the start. He liked working with other people, but the firm culture placed a higher value on working against them. When he tried to take a more collaborative approach with opposing counsel, the partners came down on him hard. He was miserable, and started having panic attacks. He had started going to group therapy at NYU while he was still in law school. Those sessions became invaluable while he was at Sullivan & Cromwell. "The group was my refuge for five years," he says. He also started seeing an individual therapist, whose work he admired so much that he started to reconsider his brother's career advice.

But he needed to get out of law first. The firm helped him with that. As a consequence of his misery, Will stopped performing at work as well as he had when he started. His supervisors noticed, and suggested that perhaps Sullivan & Cromwell was not the right place for him. "Thank goodness I got fired," he says. The firm paid for him to see an outplacement counselor.

Because Will knew so little about what other jobs involved, the counselor suggested that he do some informational interviews. At the time, Will knew little about networking, and it didn't come naturally to him. His outplacement counselor pushed him to develop those skills, a coercive approach that was exactly what he needed at the time.

In all, he had forty-one informational interviews. As Will thought about what he might want to do, he kept thinking about books. He started to focus his outreach on people who had something to do with publishing. His networking led him to his next job: a junior marketing position at Barnes & Noble. "And after that, I had a new identity," he says.

The persuasive skills Will had honed in law school helped him get his first marketing job. Although Barnes & Noble was initially resistant to hiring someone with Will's legal background, he convinced them that he was a great bargain. Because he wanted the job so much, he told them that he would be very flexible about his salary. He also pointed out that they could probably halve their legal bills by hiring him, since he could review contracts in-house. They gave him a chance.

Will's starting salary at Barnes & Noble was half of what he had been making at Sullivan & Cromwell. He had a more junior title, but his work was more engaging. Will liked the process of brainstorming with corporate partners like MBNA and Master-Card to come up with deals that worked well for everyone. Will was soon known as the person who could make corporate relationships work, and he could draft agreements quickly himself. His creative approach was praised instead of punished.

Although he was doing well at Barnes & Noble, something was still missing. One night, his brother noticed that Will seemed to be bored with his work, in spite of his success. "He asked me whether I really cared if the company's revenue was up or down," says Will. "And that cut through me. I was at Barnes & Noble only because I liked books, but I didn't care at all about selling them." For the second time since law school, he set out to change careers.

Will wasn't afraid to ask for support. "I told a friend that I needed someone to remind me who I was, and that I was unique and skilled," he says. "He told me that I was a good listener. I knew that on some level, but it helped to hear it from someone else."

What Will really valued, he realized, was people and personal relationships. Leaving the firm for Barnes & Noble had been a good first step, but it hadn't put him on the path he really wanted to follow. After talking with many therapists, including his brother, he decided to become a therapist himself.

In order to do so, he had to go back to school for a two-year program. He took on another $35,000 of debt to go to Hunter College School of Social Work, which was a fraction of what he would have owed had he gone to a private university. "I highly recommend cheap schools," he says. Returning to school in his thirties, he was quite a bit older than most of his class-mates. He also had to work at an unpaid internship for two years. He found it hard to be as deferential as his internship required, and at one point he was almost thrown out.

When Will graduated, he got a part-time job at a clinic, earn-ing less than $27,000. He taught ten-week group sessions at the clinic, filling the seats primarily by word of mouth. After his clients completed the group sessions, he offered to see them individually through his own practice. His fee, set deliberately low at first, rose over time. After five or six years in practice, he was making a six-figure salary again.

But he is not in it to get rich, he says. He is in it to be happy, and he is. After all, he says, "What would you pay if I could guar-antee you would be happy about what you were doing all day?"

Some of Will's clients now are unhappy lawyers. He empa-thizes with the difficulty some of them have in seeing outside the world of the firm. "Law firms can be hermetic," he says, "and it's easy to get tunnel vision." When everyone you know is a lawyer, he says, it can be hard to see that not everyone works on weekends. His lawyer clients, he notes, often try to rationalize their unhappiness at work by telling him that it is "just a job."

Will disagrees. He believes that work is a form of self-expression critical to living a good life. "It's important to find the work you love to do, but you need to look inside to do so," he says. "Everyone deserves to get up in the morning and go to a job they are excited about. It is a right."

16

THE INDEPENDENT

You never know what's going to lead to your next career. For Alan Rilla, it was reading a newspaper article in the *Boston Globe* about an island that needed a caretaker. He had the time to read the article while he was recovering from a broken neck, an injury he sustained after a group of prisoners threw him off a balcony. Alan was at the prison doing some of the corrections work that shaped his second career. His first career was practicing law, initially as an assistant district attorney and then in private practice.

Alan's story illustrates two important points. First, life-changing opportunities come in some unusual forms, like a broken neck and a newspaper article. Second, you should never underestimate how qualified you may be to do an interesting job that seems wholly unrelated to your legal career. Alan was selected for the island caretaker job from among sixty applicants, many of whom had more direct experience with islands and boats, in part because of his project management experience, problem-solving skills, and general intelligence. His incredible charisma probably had something to do with it, too.

Alan Rilla, Island Caretaker

When people ask Alan Rilla, caretaker of Spectacle Island, how to get a job like his, he laughs and tells them, "You can't." Alan, a former lawyer and corrections specialist, has been responsible for overseeing this Boston Harbor island since 2006. It's a job he applied for, along with sixty other people, after reading an article about the open position in the *Boston Globe*. He describes it as "the best job in America." For six months of the year he has the island more or less to himself. During the other six months, he entertains as many as eighty-five thousand visitors from all over the world.

Alan grew up in a close-knit Italian neighborhood in the Berkshires. An internship in the Public Defenders' Office after college got him interested in law. His decision to go to law school was a big deal not only for his family, but for his entire community. Most people never left his neighborhood.

After law school, Alan spent a few years with the district attorney's office. He was in court all the time, which he loved. One day, another lawyer came up to him in court and asked when Alan was "going to give this up and start making some real money." A lunch meeting led to some interviews with one of the most prestigious firms in Berkshire County, and Alan joined its practice. His first client became the most lucrative in the firm's history. Alan had a pretty comfortable life mostly serving that one client for fifteen years. But his father pointed out its shortcomings.

As Alan describes it, "When I was a Master of the Universe, and had moved into a big house, my father would come by and say, 'You know what the problem is with this big house and all these toys you love?' I'd say, 'No, what's the problem with all these things I worked so hard for?' And he'd say, 'They can't love you back.'"

When his father started to show early signs of Alzheimer's, Alan thought about that conversation. His main client had just been acquired by a larger company. He decided to downsize, and resigned his partnership. Although it was a hard decision, he knew it was the right one. A mentor pointed out that Alan had had a tremendous run. He had been practicing law for sixteen years and had never been sued or reported to the Bar. His mentor told him, "If you no longer have the fire in your belly for law, you should get out now, because you may start making mistakes."

Alan spent the last two years of his father's life caring for him, and then turned his attention to other projects. An opportunity to testify at the Massachusetts State House on reforms to the corrections system led to an opportunity to work with Sheriff Michael Ash, whom Alan had admired for a long time. Alan spent eight years working in the corrections system, developing juvenile justice programs that won multi-million-dollar federal grants and became models for other states. Although he took a substantial pay cut to do it, it was more gratifying than anything he had done before.

His corrections center work allowed him to channel his talents toward an issue he was passionate about. He used his legal experience and writing skills to get new corrections centers funded. Those centers had an enormous impact on their communities. One of the projects he developed is the Juvenile Resource Center in Pittsfield, Massachusetts, a collaboration among the Pittsfield School Department, the Berkshire Juvenile Court, and the Berkshire County Sheriff's Office.

A serious injury led to his next career change. In March 2005, his attempt to calm down a disturbance at the jail didn't go as planned. A group of rowdy inmates threw him off a second-story balcony, breaking his neck. "I took the broken neck as a sign that it was time for me to do something else," he says.

His recovery and rehabilitation took months. Nearly a year after his injury, he read an article in the *Boston Globe* about the Spectacle Island caretaker job. The article noted that applicants needed to have their own boats. He happened to have one, so he applied. He was fifty-two at the time.

A few weeks later, he received a call asking him to come to the island for an interview. Alan, who had never formally interviewed for anything in his life, agreed to go. When he got to the pier, he realized that all sixteen of the "final cut" applicants had been asked to come at the same time. "It was like being on *American Idol*," he says.

The other candidates also had impressive backgrounds. One was a Harvard professor. Another was a lifelong sailor. Some other candidates had devoted their lives to the Boston Harbor islands in one way or another. "I didn't know there were islands in the harbor until I applied," Alan notes. One of the candidates brought his wife, who worked for Boston Mayor Thomas Menino. While he interviewed, she went into the caretaker's apartment and started measuring all the rooms. "We all thought it was over at that point," he says.

But it wasn't. When Alan got the offer a week later, he asked the caller if he was sure he had the right person. The caller told Alan that the hiring committee's decision had been unanimous. Alan started work on the island in April 2006.

The best part of his job, he says, is the people who visit the island from all over the world. He has become friendly with families who come back every year, and has watched their kids grow up. "I am so excited about my job," he says. "I feel like doing cartwheels and backflips every day in the Visitor's Center."

Alan is not sure what he'll do when his term ends in 2016. The uncertainty doesn't bother him at all. He's confident that more good things will happen. "I just don't know whether they'll be on Spectacle Island or not."

Even though Alan's story doesn't fit into any of the eight alternative career paths laid out in this book, it is too interesting not to tell. It is also an important reminder that every ex-lawyer follows a unique path to a more rewarding career. Many other ex-lawyers have fascinating and uncategorizable transitions. Their personal passions and the unpredictable circumstances of their lives create opportunities for more joy than they would ever have had if they had stayed in law. They are grateful for the chance to start again and for their deeply satisfying new careers. I hope you will become one of them.

ENDNOTES

PART I

1. Martin Seligman, *Authentic Happiness: Using the New Positive Psychology to Realize Your Potential for Lasting Fulfillment* (New York: Free Press, 2002), 177.

Chapter 1

1. Lincoln Caplan, "An Existential Crisis for Law Schools," *New York Times*, July 14, 2012.
2. Jennifer Smith, "Law-Firm Partners Face Layoffs," *Wall Street Journal*, January 6, 2013.
3. Karen Sloan, "Law School Enrollment Continues Its Decline," *National Law Journal*, November 28, 2012.

Chapter 3

1. *Report of the Seventh Annual NAWL National Survey on Retention and Promotion of Women in Law Firms*, October 2012, 6.
2. *Harvard Law School Program on the Legal Profession C55 Survey Results*, October 2008, 6–7.
3. Fiona Kay and Elizabeth Gorman, "Women in the Legal Profession," *Annual Review of Law and Social Science* 2008.4:299-332, 301, 306.

REFERENCES

Caplan, Lincoln. "An Existential Crisis for Law Schools." *New York Times,* July 14, 2012.

Harvard Law School Program on the Legal Profession C55 Survey Results, October 2008.

Kay, Fiona, and Elizabeth Gorman. "Women in the Legal Profession." Annual Review of Law and Social Science, 2008.

Report of the Seventh Annual NAWL National Survey on Retention and Promotion of Women in Law Firms, October 2012.

Seligman, Martin. *Authentic Happiness: Using the New Positive Psychology to Realize Your Potential for Lasting Fulfillment.* New York: Free Press, 2002.

Sloan, Karen. "Law School Enrollment Continues Its Decline." *National Law Journal,* November 28, 2012.

Smith, Jennifer. "Law-Firm Partners Face Layoffs." *Wall Street Journal,* January 6, 2013.